FORUM AT ROME

THE METAPHORS OF ST. PAUL AND COMPANIONS OF ST. PAUL

BY

JOHN S. HOWSON, D. D.

DEAN OF CHESTER

WITH AN INTRODUCTION

BY

PROF. H. B. HACKETT, D. D.

EDITOR OF SMITH'S BIBLE DICTIONARY

TWO VOLUMES IN ONE

PUBLISHED BY THE

AMERICAN TRACT SOCIETY

117 WASHINGTON STREET, BOSTON

HURD AND HOUGHTON, 13 ASTOR PLACE, N. Y.

The Riverside Press, Cambridge, Mass

1872.

RIVERSIDE, CAMBRIDGE:
STEREOTYPED AND PRINTED BY
H. O. HOUGHTON AND COMPANY.

INTRODUCTION.

THE name of Dr. Howson, author of the tracts in this volume, needs no introduction to American readers. His writings, especially his "Life and Epistles of Paul" and his "Hulsean Lectures on the Character of Paul," have made him as well known in this country as in England. Even in these more elaborate works he has shown a rare faculty of so treating his subjects as to interest and instruct readers of every class.

The tracts here published are an outgrowth of these more extended studies to which we have referred. The one on the "Metaphors of Paul" consists of papers first published in the "Sunday Magazine" in England (1866–67), and republished at the instance of the present writer in the American "Theological Eclectic" (1867–68). The papers were subsequently brought together by the author himself in a book form and published in England in 1870. They are reprinted here from that edition.

The contents are adapted to the wants of the general reader, as well as of the student and the preacher. The "Metaphors" of Paul are a part of his writings that specially need such illustration. The Apostle James derives his most expressive figures from natural objects, or from permanent aspects of human life and experience;[1] and hence they are readily understood without comment or explanation in every age and by every people. The Apostle Paul has taken his imagery largely from local customs and national usages which for us have passed away; and hence the allusions to them can be fully understood only as the things themselves are explained and set before us by vivid representation. This service Dr. Howson has performed for us in an admirable manner. He gives us no tedious archæological details; but just the requisite kind and amount of information concerning the military and agricultural usages of the Greeks and Romans, their style of architecture, and the contests of the gymnasium and stadium; and thus we are enabled to see and feel almost as eye-witnesses the force of his illustrations drawn from such sources. The study of Paul's Metaphors as unfolded in these pages reveals a striking unity in his Epistles, and they help to confirm their genuineness. It should be mentioned, too, that our English Version often fails to bring out the full significance of these fig-

1 See, for example, the Epistle of James, i. 6, 10; iii. 4, 5, 7; iv. 14; v. 2, 3, 7, etc.

ures. Dr. Howson has taken pains to correct these inaccuracies, and has thus restored to the reader some of the most expressive traits of Paul's imagery, otherwise lost to us. It is surprising to find how much new beauty and instructiveness are often given to the Apostle's language by such corrections.

The crowning excellence of the work, after all, is its practical aim and earnest religious spirit. Its ample learning, its illustrations, its eloquence, are all subordinate to that end. It is adapted to stimulate religious feeling, and to impress the truth, as well as guide us to a knowledge of it.

In speaking of the other work, the "Sketches of Paul's Companions," a brief word may suffice.

The notices of the Apostle's co-laborers who appear in the Acts and the Epistles, are so scattered and incidental that the ordinary reader seldom obtains a distinct idea of their number or of their characteristics and individuality. Dr. Howson has brought together these fugitive notices in his "Sketches" so as to present the actors in their separate fields of labor as well as in their coördination to the great Apostle: and has thus given us a juster impression both of the manifold labors of these Companions of Paul and of his own greater efficiency from his having had such coadjutors. Dr. Howson's familiarity with this branch of Scripture history is shown here to great advantage.

H. B. H.

CONTENTS.

THE METAPHORS OF ST. PAUL.

THE

METAPHORS OF ST. PAUL.

I.

ROMAN SOLDIERS.

EVERY part of Holy Scripture has its own distinctive imagery; and through the medium of this imagery its instruction is often conveyed. Thus, when we read the prophecies of Amos, "who was among the herdmen of Tekoa,"—himself a "herdman" in a wild and pastoral district,—the images are such as these: the fat "kine of Bashan, which say unto their masters, Bring and let us drink;" "the lion roaring in the forest;" "the seven stars of Orion, before the shadow of death is turned into the morning;" "the basket of summer fruit;" "the grasshoppers in the shooting up of the latter growth." Unless we rightly apprehend the circumstances, the scenery, and the pursuits, in connection with which it was God's will that His prophet should speak, we cannot fully understand the meaning of His words; and so far, to us, their force and instructiveness is diminished.

The imagery of the Book of Amos is an emphatic

and strongly marked instance of a principle which is applicable, in various degrees, to all parts of the Bible. The life of Joseph, the life of Moses, the life of Ruth, the life of Elijah, all have their appropriate atmosphere and coloring; and if we look at them without reference to these, they fade away into something abstract and dead. And so it is with the New Testament. But here, though the principle is the same, we feel that we are brought into a new world, and that the principle must be applied to very different details. Every part of the Old Testament has an oriental complexion. We illustrate it by referring to what travellers tell us of the tents of the Bedouin Arabs, of the courts of Eastern princes, of caravans and camels and palm trees. And so it is, no doubt, to some extent, in the case of the New Testament. But still, on the whole, in passing from one to the other, we are conscious that a change has come over the scene, and that God has begun to speak to us now through similitudes of a different kind. We find ourselves brought in contact with circumstances far more nearly resembling those which surround us in modern life. We are in fact, when the New Testament is our study, on the borders or in the heart of Greek civilization, and we are always in the midst of the Roman Empire. It is no more possible fully to understand what the Apostles say to us, than what the Prophets say to us, if we dissever their words from the circumstances of their lives. The metaphors they use are drawn (as indeed they must have been drawn, to be intelligible at all) from the things which were around them. My endeavor will be, in four sections, to illustrate certain groups of images which are common in one part of the New Testament, and, in the present section, while keeping in view especially one very notable passage in the Epistle to the Ephesians, to elucidate *the military metaphors of St. Paul.*

It seldom occurs to us to consider how large a portion of his time St. Paul spent in the close proximity of soldiers. He lived under the shadow of the greatest military monarchy which the world has seen. Englishmen are less able than others to realize all that is implied in this simple fact; hence they are startled into the impression of novelty, when they first travel in France or Austria, and see troops filing through the streets of every city, and large barracks in every country town. But such sights were no novelty to St. Paul. No doubt they were more frequent and conspicuous in some parts of the Empire than others. In Philippi, for instance, in Troas, and the Pisidian Antioch, which were Roman colonies, we may well believe that the warlike symbols of Rome were more prominent than in other cities which he visited; and the State of Syria, which was a very uneasy province, and was held by a standing army of 60,000 men, was very different from that of Achaia or Bithynia, which were comparatively quiet and settled districts. But, wherever he resided, military uniforms and military quarters were familiar objects; wherever he travelled, he was liable to meet troops on their march from one province to another, or in the pursuit of banditti, or acting as an escort of prisoners.

But we are not left to this general kind of illustration. We are well acquainted with several incidents of his life, which connected him, in a manner peculiarly intimate, with Roman soldiers and their officers and their armor. It is enough to make a simple reference to his arrest in the court of the Temple, when the commandant of the garrison of Antonia with some of his subalterns and a body of troops, ran down and took him into custody, — then to the time which the Apostle spent in the barracks within Antonia, and to the events which took place there, — then to his night journey to Antipatris, under the charge of a guard almost as numerous as half an English regiment, besides a squadron of dragoons, — then to his captivity of two years at Cæsarea, the centre of the provincial military government, where he was probably chained by the hand to a soldier, — then to his adventurous voyage, when an officer of a distinguished corps was his close companion, and when the swords of the soldiers under his command, which had cut the fastenings of the boat, were only just prevented from taking the Apostle's life and the lives of his fellow-prisoners, — then to the delivering up of the prisoners to the commander of the Prætorian Guards, after which, though Paul was suffered to dwell by himself, yet it was not without "a soldier who kept him," — and lastly, to the facts hinted at in passages of the Epistles written at Rome, as when he says, in affixing his autograph to the Colossian letter, "the salutation by the hand of me Paul," and then, feeling the chain clank on his wrist as he writes, he adds, "remember my chains," — or, in the Ephesian letter, when he describes himself as "an ambassador in bonds," — an ambassador of the free Gospel, fastened to a soldier; — it is enough to enumerate these things, in order to see how natural it is that St. Paul should speak to us in military metaphors, nay, how unnatural it would be (if I may say so with reverence) were no such metaphors to be found in his writings.

Our best mode of approaching the direct illustration of our selected context is first to notice some of those other texts where imagery of the same kind is more lightly touched by St. Paul, and so to rise by successive steps to the allegory in which the Christian warrior is set before us in the full panoply of God. Then it will not be irrelevant if we turn in conclusion to some other passages, where similes from the same source are employed by the Apostle, less obviously but not less forcibly.

The first of these passages is in the thirteenth chapter of the Romans.[1] That Epistle was written at Corinth, which, both as the seat of local government, and because of its critical position on a strait between two seas, must have been garrisoned by a strong military force. The image which always rises before my mind when I read the passage, is this: I

[1] Rom. xiii. 11–13.

fancy St. Paul — after a day spent in hard work, partly in tent-making and partly in preaching and in visitation among his converts — writing far through the night to the Christians in Rome, and just at day-break, when the sentinels are changing guard, and the morning light glances on their armor, — while at the same time the last sounds of debauched revelers in the street fall upon his ears, — expressing himself in the now familiar words, "The night is far spent, the day is at hand; let us therefore cast off the works of darkness, and let us put on *the armor of light;* let us walk honestly as in the day, not in rioting and drunkenness."

As to the phrase "armor of light," it is evidently equivalent to the phrase "*armor of righteousness,*" which he uses elsewhere,[1] — *i. e.*, spiritual armor for the contest against spiritual foes. But in the place where this last expression occurs, the idea is more fully developed than in the former case. Here it is "the armor of righteousness on the right hand and on the left." We have not simply armor in the abstract, as in the other instance, but armor specially described as of two kinds, "*on the right hand and on the left,*" — *i. e.*, offensive and defensive, represented generally by the sword and the shield. St. Paul is here describing himself, and his own attitude in regard to the resistance he had met with at Corinth in the progress of his apostolic work. This is not the only occasion in this severe Epistle (as we shall

[1] 2 Cor. vi. 7.

see afterwards) where he uses military language in describing his own position in reference to the enemies of the truth.

We reach something still more definite and specific, when we come to the fifth chapter of the first letter to the Thessalonians.[1] "We are not of the night . . . . therefore let us not sleep . . . They that be drunken, are drunken in the night. . . . Let us, who are of the day, be sober, putting on the breastplate of faith and love; and for an helmet, the hope of salvation." The chief remarks to be made here, I think, are that this Epistle was written from Corinth, like that to the Romans, but on a previous visit; that the whole context is very similar to that which has been quoted from the Romans; and that while this passage contains many more details than that just adduced from the second Corinthian Epistle, yet it is entirely limited to defensive armor. As to any observations on two pieces of armor that are specified, — "the *breastplate* of faith and love," and the "*helmet* of salvation," — these belong more properly to our discussion of the allegory in the sixth of Ephesians,[1] which claims from us now a more direct consideration.

Enough has been quoted already to prove that the use of military metaphors is a familiar thing to St. Paul. And in the passages hitherto adduced, these metaphors have one general type, which is quite in harmony with the longer extract before us. In ex-

[1] 1 Thess. v. 5–8. [1] Eph. vi. 10–17.

amining its different parts, I should wish to be guided by the reverent belief that each word has a meaning, — that each word is the best that could be used, — and at the same time, I should wish to be on my guard against that pedantry of interpretation which tortures the Bible into meanings which it was never intended to bear, and which, in this case, would deprive the Apostle's imagery of all its freshness and elasticity.

I have called the passage an allegory. But it cannot strictly be described by that term. It is a series of images with a running explanation. In a pure allegory the key of interpretation is to be derived from the context, or from the circumstances, or from analogy. But here the image and the interpretation are given side by side. We "wrestle" or engage in close conflict, but "not with flesh and blood," — *i. e.*, (as we see from a passage where the same phrase is used in the Galatians), not with man, but with spiritual foes. We wear "armor," but it is the armor of light, the armor of righteousness, the panoply of God. We carry a "shield," but it is the shield of faith. We wield a "sword," but it is the sword of the Spirit. This is St. Paul's manner. He explains his metaphors as he proceeds. We have, therefore, no need to waste our time discussing the principles of the interpretation of allegory. We may begin at once to go in order through the clauses of which the passage is composed.

One of the first thoughts which occur to us in looking at the introductory words is this, that the armor is of no use to us unless we put it on. We are not to be passive in the matter. The opening words give a positive injunction; and the only way to obey the injunction is to put on the armor, and to wear it and use it. Another obvious thought relates to the perilous condition of those who are destitute of this armor. Without it we are utterly defenseless. And it is no light matter to be defenseless in the presence of a foe, who is not only hostile but accomplished in stratagem, and who commands an army such as that which is described in the verses before us. There is a story of a Spartan soldier who went into battle without his armor, and who was fined by the Senate though he had been victorious. This anecdote supplies a very useful admonition to the Christian soldier.

One word in this introductory portion is unfortunately translated in the Authorized Version. The phrase, "having done all," is by no means, in my opinion, an adequate rendering of the Greek. The marginal translation, "having *overcome*," is more correct. The original denotes that we are to beat down all opposition, and having done this to "stand," to hold our ground. And this word "*stand*," which occurs once and again, sets before us the true nature of the Christian's conflict. We have a defensive military position to hold for God, and we must hold it. Our duty is no light skirmish which might be half an amusement to those who enjoy a fray; but it is a serious and momentous struggle to hold the field where we are posted, like the struggle of those who fought at Inkermann.

I find in two of Chrysostom's sermons on this chapter some remarks on these introductory verses so good and forcible that I think they deserve to be quoted. With reference to the wiles of the devil he expresses himself as follows: "The Apostle saith not, Against the *fighting*, nor Against the *hostilities*, but Against the *wiles*. This enemy is at war with us, not simply, not openly, but by wiles: *i. e.*, he tries to deceive us and to take us by artifice. He never proposes to us sins in their proper colors. Thus, he does not speak of idolatry, but he sets it off in another dress, making his discourse plausible, and employing disguises." In reference to the expression just alluded to, "having subdued all," he adds: "That is, having subdued our passions and vile lusts, and all things else that trouble us. The Apostle speaks not merely of doing the deed, but of completing it, so as not only to slay, but to stand after we have slain; for many who have gained this victory have failed again. *Having subdued all*, saith he, not *Having subdued one and not another;* for even after the victory we must stand. An enemy may be struck, but things that are struck revive again." And once more, in reference to the word "stand," Chrysostom says: "The very first feature in tactics is to know how to stand well, and many things will depend upon that. In the case of mere athletic exercises the word of command which the trainer gives before anything else is this, to stand firm. Much more will it be the first thing in military matters. The man who, in a true sense, stands, is upright; he stands not in a lazy attitude, not leaning upon anything. The luxurious man does not stand upright, but stoops; so does the lewd man, so does the lover of money."

This is enough concerning the *attitude and posture* of the Christian warrior. We come now to *the armor itself* which he wears. As described to us here we observe that it consists of six pieces. A few words may be devoted to each of them. But first let us bear in mind how much reality and life are communicated to the description when we recollect where St. Paul was when he wrote it. He was in the midst of the Prætorian Guards, the *élite* of the Roman army, a body of men raised far more conspicuously above the legions than our Guards, or even the French Imperial Guard, are above the regiments of the line. But not only was he in the midst of them, seeing them continually, and hearing daily all the sounds of barrack life, but he was fastened to one of these guardsmen while he dictated the letter, and he felt the chain on his wrist while he affixed his signature.

First in order of enumeration we have the BELT — "having your loins girt about with *truth*." By this we are not to understand a loose sword-belt like that which our own officers wear, nor any ornamented girdle, but a very strong girding apparatus, made of leather and covered with metal plates, and fastened firmly round the loins. The appearance and use of it are best seen in ancient statues in the British Museum and elsewhere. It was the first part of the armor which the soldier would put on, and it was of essential use to him for the purpose of safety, and especially for the sake of standing firmly. It was to the Roman soldier exactly what Truth is to the soldier of Christ. Of Christ Himself it is said in the prophecy, that "righteousness shall be the girdle of his loins, and faithfulness" (the word is *truth* in the Septuagint) "the girdle of his reins." [1]

The BREASTPLATE is next to be considered. It is described as the "breastplate of *righteousness*." A question might be raised here as to the meaning of the word "righteousness," whether it denotes the justification which belongs to the believer by virtue of his union with Christ, or refers to that rectitude of character which cannot be wanting in a true Christian. I feel little doubt that the latter is the true meaning of St. Paul; and this for two or three reasons. In the first place justification would seem to belong more naturally to the "shield of faith," which is mentioned below; but, again, it appears to me that all the parts of defensive armor mentioned here designate graces of Christian character. Moreover, in the shorter allegory of the first Thessalonian letter the breastplate is described as made up of "faith and love," a perfect account of that principle in a Christian which leads him to feel rightly, to think rightly,

[1] Isaiah xi. 5.

and to act rightly; but hardly such a definition as we should expect of a sinner's state of pardon and acceptance with God. But there is another reason which, to my mind, is almost decisive. St. Paul is here again using Greek words from the Old Testament (and it is important to observe this; for there is seldom any long passage in St. Paul's writings without some quotation from the Septuagint), and there we find it said of the Lord Himself that "He put on righteousness as a breastplate, and an helmet of salvation on his head."[1] The incongruity is obvious on the former interpretation. "It is God that justifieth."

This reference to Isaiah leads me to break the order of St. Paul's words, and to take "the helmet of *salvation*" next after the "breastplate of righteousness;" for they are coupled together in the same clause by the prophet from whom he quotes. Clearly we might have some difficulty here in assigning a precise meaning to the Christian's helmet, were it not that the Apostle himself comes to our assistance; for he says to the Thessalonians that it is "the *hope* of salvation" which we are to take for a HELMET. I conceive, then, that we are to see here a representation of that cheerful and courageous hope which is so important an element in the Christian's warfare, and so bright an ornament and crowning point to all the other graces of his character.

The helmet is perhaps the brightest and most con-

[1] Isaiah lix. 17.

spicuous part of a soldier's equipment; but there are other parts less showy, but not less essential. A soldier badly shod can never last well through a campaign. Many of us have a vivid remembrance of what we read in the newspapers concerning some passages of the Crimean War. St. Paul does not leave his description of the Christian warrior incomplete in this respect. "HAVE YOUR FEET SHOD," he says, "with *the preparation* (or with the prompt ready movement) *of the gospel of peace.*" It is needless to enter here into any details concerning the military equipment of the feet which enabled the Roman armies to march to the conquest of the world; but we should observe the holy irony with which St. Paul gives an unexpected turn to his mention of this part of the Christian armor. The Roman soldiers were all on the alert in obeying orders to carry into every nation the miseries of *War.* The like alacrity ought to be shown by us in our obedience to our Captain; and no slipshod indolence ought to make us slow in moving on this happy errand of *Peace.*

The words in which the Authorized Version introduces the SHIELD are again (I conceive) inadequate, or, at least, obscure. "Above all" conveys the impression of "especially," as though the Apostle were now about to mention what is most important. And perhaps "the shield of faith" is, in fact, the most important of all the defenses of the Christian soldier. But I think the Greek words mean simply "over all," "on the outside of all." The great Roman shield referred to here was very different from the small bucklers which were used in some kinds of ancient warfare. Sculptured representations of it may be seen on Trajan's Column. It covered and protected the whole body; and whatever weak points there might be in other parts of the armor, this supplied their deficiencies, as faith comes to the rescue when all other graces are failing. True faith is invaluable and invulnerable. It is competent to quench even the "fiery arrows" of the Evil One. Here the image of the Christian conflict assumes all the animation of a *siege;* and one of the best illustrations I am acquainted with of the words used by the Apostle is in the history of one of the sieges of Rhodes, during which arrows charged with combustible materials were sent against the ships, and the very expression chosen here by St. Paul is employed by Diodorus Siculus in describing the defenses used for quenching the fire.

One part of the armor remains — THE SWORD — "the sword of the Spirit, which is the Word of God," — *i. e.*, the sword which the Spirit gives, and which is none other than God's revealed truth. This is the one offensive weapon. We are not sanctioned in the use of any other; all the rest of our armor is defensive; and this is very instructive. Our conflict is not with man, but with sin. We have no angry passions of our own to gratify. Our duty is steadfastly to resist; and when we strike, we must strike only with the weapon which God puts into our hands. All this is made more emphatic, if we observe that one weapon, — the most characteristic weapon of the Roman soldier, — the great *pilum* or pike, which Lord Macaulay has introduced with strict truth into one of his "Lays of Rome," — this weapon is entirely omitted. Here the parallel is left incomplete. Can we doubt that this was done purposely? The silence of Scripture has its meaning as well as its actual words.

I abstain from further and closer practical comments. These would enter into the region of Christian experience, and would belong to a treatise of a deeper kind. I will only now, through a few remaining paragraphs, follow the same thread of thought, where it conducts us to one or two other places, in which (as I have said) military metaphors are employed, less obviously at first sight, though not less forcibly.

Some of these relate to the long operation of *campaigning*, rather than the mere putting on of armor. Thus, when Timotheus is admonished to "endure hardness as a good soldier of Jesus Christ," it is added by the Apostle: "No man that goeth on a campaign entangleth himself with the common affairs of life, that he may please him who hath chosen him to be a soldier."[1] It is to be regretted that the expression "*this* life" should have found a place in the English Version, inasmuch as it mixes the metaphor with the thing intended, besides stating what is not

[1] 2 Tim. ii. 3, 4.

true. For if one thing above all others belongs peculiarly to this life, it is War. This, however, does not hinder war, in the form of a prolonged campaign, from furnishing most apt illustrations of three things which are expected from the Christian, — patient endurance, firm separation from those interests which are not compatible with his main purpose, and an earnest desire to please his Commander.

There is again a passage in the early part of the Second Epistle to the Corinthians,[1] which involves no difficulty as to its general meaning, but great part of the vividness of which we lose by not noticing how imagery, drawn from the conduct of a campaign, runs through the whole of the context. In the last passage the reference was to an individual soldier; here it is to a commander. St. Paul is speaking in peremptory language of his apostolic power and authority. The military phraseology starts suddenly to view in the third verse, "Though we walk in the flesh, we do not war after the flesh." This is clear enough. But in what follows it is not always remarked that every phrase to the end of the sixth verse is appropriate to some part of a campaign, and drawn in fact from the familiar experience of those terrible Roman wars which were well remembered in every region through which the Apostle travelled. No one will question this as regards the words "weapons," and "warfare." But the "strongholds" are the rock forts, such as those which once bristled

[1] 2 Cor. x. 3–6.

along the coast of his native Cilicia, and of which he must often have heard, when his father told him how they were "pulled down" by the Romans in their wars against the pirates. Those "high things that exalt themselves," those high eminences of the pride of nature, occupied in force by hostile troops, had been a familiar experience in many wars throughout Asia Minor, while one of the grandest of all was the Acropolis that towered over Corinth. But this is not all. Ancient warfare ended with the taking of prisoners, who were carried into some safe place (such as this very Acropolis) where obedience would be secure. So the Apostle speaks of "bringing into captivity every thought to (or rather *into*) the obedience of Christ." And then, further, if in a country that had been conquered on the whole, rebellions were here and there to break out again, it was not the habit of the Romans to desist till complete subordination was established. So the Apostle holds himself in readiness to "revenge all disobedience," even when on the whole (for this he will not doubt) the general "obedience" of the Corinthian Church is "fulfilled." Here then are a series of phrases which describe the vigorous prosecution of a campaign, and the determined subjugation of the last symptom of rebellion. And who will say that we do not lose by failing to notice this character of the language? Who will say that we do not gain by allowing it to have its natural and close association with what history tells of the course and the consolidation of Roman military conquest?

And more yet remains to be said concerning even this portion of the subject. St. Paul pursues the progress of the campaign till it reaches that which, in a Roman's eyes, was the most glorious of all consummations, — the progress of the triumphal procession after final victory; and he introduces God Himself as the victor and the leader of the triumph. Twice we find this image expressed, with the technical and classical word which belongs to the subject: once when the great conquest effected through the death of Christ is the topic of the Apostle's enthusiastic sentences,[1] and once when the progressive advance of the Gospel of Christ is represented in language strictly suitable to the long procession of conqueror and captives by the Sacred Way to the Capitol.[2] In the former case the words are brief and simple, which describe the "open display" of the defeat of "principalities and powers." In the latter the description is prolonged and given in detail. The doctrine preached by the Apostle "in every place" is compared to the fragrance which filled the streets from clouds of incense; while the fatal doom of the captives contrasted with the exulting joy of the citizens, is a vivid representation of the awful alternative which separates the hearers of the Gospel into "them that are saved," and "them that perish."

And still the whole subject of the military metaphors of St. Paul is not exhausted. There are other passages where the same expressive imagery occurs:

[1] Col. ii. 15. [1] 2 Cor. ii. 14–16.

as when he tells us that "without were *fightings*, within were fears," a description of his own experience which may well give encouragement to us;[1] or as when he speaks of the "law in our members *waging war* against the law of the mind and taking us captive;" and perhaps our own experience is enough to make us aware that no metaphor would be more suitable to the case than one derived from the dreadful realities of war;[2] or as when he assures his most consistent converts that "the *peace* of God, which passeth all understanding, shall *garrison* their hearts and minds through Christ Jesus."[3] This is an unexpected — almost an ironical — turn, like that which we noticed before, when we saw that "the preparation of the Gospel of peace" was an essential part of the "armor of God." And the natural conclusion of these remarks is an allusion to the Great Resurrection, when "*the trumpet shall sound*,"[4] and every faithful Christian warrior shall have his place in his own "order" or "*division*," of the vast Army of the Lord of Hosts.[5]

1 2 Cor. vii. 5. 2 Rom. vii. 23. 3 Phil. iv. 7.
4 1 Cor. xv. 52; see xiv. 8. 5 1 Cor. xv. 23.

II.

CLASSICAL ARCHITECTURE.

OUR last section was on the military metaphors of St. Paul, with especial reference to the middle portion of the sixth chapter of the Epistle to the Ephesians. The present will deal with the *architectural metaphors* of the same Apostle, with prominent but not by any means exclusive reference to a passage in the third chapter of the Second Epistle to the Corinthians.

The thought which lies at the basis of these essays is this: that in order to understand an ancient writer it is not enough to study his books, but necessary also to know something of the fashion of his times, — not safe simply to work from the Dictionary, without some regard to the records of Monumental History, without some effort to reproduce and realize manners and customs, and the outward expression of the old social life. Even in order to understand the bare meaning of the words, we must know something of the life. Much more, when we desire to appreciate the nicer shades of meaning, and to enter into the full force of illustrative language. For this purpose we have need of Archæology as much as of Philology. The two cannot prudently be dissevered. And more than this. Unless our Archæology is correct, our Philology, being connected with anachronisms, will lead us into positive errors.

These observations, true of ancient writers in general, are quite as true of Sacred as Profane. Moses and Luke, Ezra and Paul, did not write independently of the circumstances with which they were surrounded, or of the tastes, pursuits, and habits of their time. If they had done so, they would have been unintelligible when they wrote. And they will only be approximately intelligible to us, unless we have the means of re-setting the words in their true associations. When a man has once seen a really Oriental city, and made himself familiar with the sights and smells of a bazaar, walked on the flat roofs, or stood among the camels, he has acquired a power of appreciating the Old Testament, such as no dead Lexicon could ever give him. And how great a help for the New Testament is gained, when, in some good museum, a man has taken into his hand a silver denarius, and looked at the fine features of Tiberius — worthy of a nobler character, — and turned the coin round, and read the Latin inscription, and reflected on the possibility that this might have been the very piece of money that was shown to our Saviour, on the high probability that it was minted at the same time, and on the certainty that it was exactly like it, in size and material, in the "image and-superscription!"

These are only superficial illustrations, but they

are illustrations of a principle; and the application of the principle becomes important, exactly in proportion as the writer in question, whoever he may be, has some favorite classes of imagery drawn from the circumstances of his time; and in proportion as those circumstances, from which the imagery is drawn, are in themselves peculiar and removed from the sphere of our own customary thoughts.

Now thus much may be said, without any danger of dispute, concerning St. Paul's favorite illustrations, that they are drawn, not from the operations and uniform phenomena of the natural world, but from the activities and outward exhibition of human society, — from the life of soldiers, the life of slaves, from the market, from athletic exercises, from agriculture, from architecture.

That there is a strong tendency to architectural metaphors in St. Paul's Epistles no one will dispute. But it is worth while to remark that this tendency to refer to buildings may be observed not only there, but in his speeches too. Let us call to mind two speeches, uttered in busy centres of population, and in the midst of those who had glorious architectural works every day before their eyes. At Athens how grandly does the Apostle point mentally, if not literally, to the Parthenon and Propylæa and their associated statues on the Acropolis, telling his hearers that God, "seeing that He is Lord of heaven and earth, dwelleth not in *temples made with hands*," and that the Godhead is not "like unto gold, or silver, or *stone*, graven by art or man's device!"[1] And at Miletus how significantly and strongly does he conclude his address to those who had come from Ephesus, where Diana's temple was the most magnificent and prominent object, — "Now, brethren, I commend you to God, and to the word of his grace, which is able to *build you up!*"[2] How or why St. Paul's style had this tendency it is needless to determine. It might be a matter of temperament or of education. He might have a taste for architecture, natural or acquired. That he was a man of fine perceptions and strong social feelings cannot be doubted. And to such men it is natural to enter into the spirit of a great city and its outward expression as given in its buildings. Again we are told that Gamaliel, under whom the Apostle was instructed, was a man of enlarged mind, and by no means destitute of sympathy with the culture of the Greeks. However this may be, St. Paul, writing under Divine inspiration, does use ideas drawn from buildings, as vehicles of instruction. Architectural phraseology is inwoven into the texture of his Epistles, and to a much larger extent than would at first sight be supposed.

Let us take, in the first place, in elucidation of this topic, a single word, the word "*edify*." This verb, or its substantive, "*edification*," occurs in some form or other about twenty times in the New Testament; and in every instance, except one, it is used by St. Paul; and that exception is in the Acts of the Apos-

1 Acts xvii. 24, 29; see verses 16 and 23. 2 Acts xx. 32.

tles,[1] a book written almost certainly under St. Paul's superintendence. This fact is remarkable, and well adapted to arrest the attention. But it becomes still more marked, when we observe that, on proceeding to look for the Greek word of which "edify" is the English translation (or rather the Latin translation, introduced from the Vulgate by Wycliffe), we find that other passages must be added to the list, and all in the same Apostle's writings. To quote the places where "edify" and "edification" occur in the English would be needless. They are all ready in our memories for use when occasion requires. But, in order to transfer our associations to the Greek word, which is actually St. Paul's word, and to which they more properly belong, I may observe that the language is precisely the same when he lays down the principle of non-interference with another Apostle's work, — "I will not build (edify) on another man's foundation;"[2] that the same favorite image occurs when he expresses the utter inconsistency involved in a return from Christianity to Judaism, — "If I proceed to build up the edifice which I took so much pains to pull down, I make myself a transgressor;"[3] and that, with regard to moral practice, he uses "build up" in a bad sense as well as a good one, when he says, after laying down the truth that it is Christian love which "builds up,"[4] that if the strong brother approaches too near association with idolatry, the

1 Acts ix. 31.
2 Rom. xv. 20.
3 Gal. ii. 18.
4 1 Cor. viii. 1.

conscience of the weak brother may be "built up,"[1] so as to eat that which is sacrificed to idols, — may become, in fact, a structure of sin. In this passage the Authorized Version has "edify" in the margin; and this is the word in Wycliffe's version. The word is "build" in the other two passages which I have just quoted. It is evident that even then the words "*edify*" and "*edification*" were narrowing themselves to their theological sense, while "*edifice*" has still continued to have its widest sense. Not that the narrowing process was completed for some considerable time. Spenser uses "edify" in the sense of building; and I find it said of the Castle of Corfu in Hakluyt's travels (under the date 1553), "It is not only of situation the strongest I have seen, but also of *edification*."

We might follow this disquisition on a single word into results of considerable interest.

The question has a bearing on *Christian Evidence*. It is something that the same prevalent metaphor is used, and in the same kind of way, in several of the Epistles which bear the name of St. Paul. Unity of style tends to prove unity of authorship. If one man wrote all these Epistles, then all are authentic. So, again, it is always interesting to find a peculiarity which marks the Epistles marking also the speeches which are assigned to this Apostle in the Acts. It helps to prove that the Paul of the letters is the Paul of the narrative; and this, too, is something. Here

[1] 1 Cor. viii. 10.

it must in candor be added, that this argument, if applied to the Epistle to the Hebrews, tends to separate it from the Epistles which were undoubtedly written by St. Paul. On some grounds, I am strongly inclined to believe that he did write the Hebrews; but this argument, so far as it goes, has a tendency the other way. In those passages, "He who hath builded the house hath more honor than the house: for every house is builded by some one; but He that built all things is God,"[1]—and "a greater and more perfect tabernacle, not of this building,"[2]—and again, "Abraham looked for a city which hath foundations, whose builder and maker is God;"[3]—in these passages it is remarkable that the original words are quite different from those which are customary with St. Paul when he speaks of building or edifying.

But again, the topic before us has a bearing on *Christian Doctrine*. I have an impression that we have acquired the habit of using the word "edify" in a way slightly different from that of St. Paul, from whom we borrow it. We give it an individual application. We say that this or that — a book read in private, a sentence from a sermon, a providential occurrence — is edifying to the individual Christian, without reference to his social position in the Church. But "edify" with St. Paul is always a social word, having regard to the mutual improvement of members of the Church, and the growth of the whole body in faith and love. "The *Churches* in Judæa

[1] Heb. iii. 3, 4. [2] Heb. ix. 11. [3] Heb. xi. 10.

and Galilee and Samaria," it is said, "had rest and were edified."[1] Paul says to the Corinthian Church, "We do all things for your edifying."[2] He says to the members of the Thessalonian Church, "Edify one another."[3] And he tells the Ephesian Church that various ministrations are given, "for the edifying of the body of Christ[4] . . . . from Whom the whole maketh increase of the body unto the edifying of itself in love."[5] So, too, he says that Christians are, collectively as well as individually, the *Temple* of God. There are two passages,[6] one in the First and one in the Second Epistle to the Corinthians, which may be instructively compared in reference to this point. Now, all this, if we consider the matter closely, is almost implied in the word, and in the metaphor which it represents. A building is an aggregate thing. And believers are not buildings, but parts of a building. St. Peter calls them "living stones." I think we are sometimes too apt to forget this, and to treat Christianity (if I may use the expression) as if it were *monolithic*. We may lose in precision by not attending to the metaphors which are involved in Scripture words, and thus the proportions of our doctrine may be disturbed. It is not too much to say that, with regard to the point before us, we might, out of St. Paul's use of the word "edify" or "build," get a whole commentary on that article of the Creed,—"I believe in the Holy Catholic Church."

[1] Acts ix. 31. [2] 2 Cor. xii. 19. [3] 1 Thess. v. 11.
[4] Eph. iv. 12. [5] Eph. iv. 16. [6] 1 Cor. vi. 19; 2 Cor. vi. 16.

However this may be, nearly all will agree that such passages as these have a very important bearing on *Christian Practice.* "All things may be lawful for me, but all things do not *edify*."[1] "We ought not to please ourselves, but let every one try to please his neighbor for his good unto *edification*."[2] "Let us follow after the things which make for peace, and things wherewith one may *edify* another."[3] The force of this last passage is much enhanced by the words which follow: "For the sake of meat do not run the risk of pulling to pieces the work — the building — of God." The word here translated "destroy" in the English version is not that which is so rendered a few verses above ("For meat destroy not him for whom Christ died"), but it is the contrasted word opposed to "build," just as in that phrase, quoted before from another Epistle (again an instance of the unity of St. Paul's style), "If I build up again what once I pulled down" or "pulled to pieces." How vividly do we see this momentous duty of respecting scruples and prejudices, of forbearance in social intercourse, of controlling our vehemence and censoriousness, when we think of those around us as parts with ourselves of a building, which ought to be advancing in beauty and solidity! Those disorderly tempers disturb the proportion, that selfishness of ours mars the unity, those hasty words, those careless acts, are the pickaxes which loosen the mortar. And so with regard to public ministrations: "He that

[1] 1 Cor. x. 23. [2] Rom. xv. 1, 2. [3] Rom. xiv. 19, 20.

speaketh in a tongue *buildeth up* himself: he that prophesieth, *buildeth up* the church;"[1] — "Forasmuch as ye are zealous of spiritual gifts, seek that ye may excel to the *building up* of the church;"[2] — "Verily thou givest thanks well, but the other is not *built up*."[3] If we neglect the principle involved in such a context as this, — if we are bent on display and power and self-advancement, — well may the Church be *dilapidated* instead of *built*. So, again, of the contrast of knowledge and love: "Knowledge inflates;" it only produces a bubble that will burst; but "love edifies," — it constructs what is solid; its work is to be patiently building a noble and enduring palace.

But it is time that we advance from words to sentences. Let us examine a few passages where the architectural metaphor is more fully developed. We will follow a natural order, and take first the foundation, then the step, and then the furniture of the house.

We have seen that St. Paul says he will not "build on another man's foundation," when he means to say that he will not trespass on another man's missionary province. But he uses the same image in a deeper sense in various emphatic passages. In two of them there is the same juxtaposition of what is agricultural and what is architectural, which we have in this third chapter of the First Epistle to the Corinthians: "Ye are God's husbandry, ye are God's building."[4] Just

[1] 1 Cor. xiv. 3–5.
[2] 1 Cor. xiv. 12.
[3] 1 Cor. xiv. 17.
[4] 1 Cor. iii. 9.

so, on turning to the Ephesians and Colossians (again an illustration of the unity of authorship), we find in one, "That ye, having your root and your *foundation* in love — your root as a tree, your foundation as a building,[1] — may be able to know what is the love of Christ;" and in the other, "As ye have received Christ so walk in Him, having your root struck down deep into Him, and raising up the building on Him as your *foundation*."[2] A glance at the Greek shows that the language is the same in both passages. The only difference is, that in the former the Ephesians are addressed as having been set on a safe foundation, the Colossians are reminded of the duty of raising up the structure so founded. Nor is this the only place in the Epistle to the Colossians where reference is made to the foundation.[3]

But let us turn to two other passages, where the imagery is presented to us in detail. Both are good illustrations of what Paley calls St. Paul's peculiarity of "going off at a word." In the nineteenth verse of the second chapter of the Ephesians, after he has happened to use the word "household," it seems as if the whole house rose before him, from foundation to roof, and transformed itself into a temple. The chapter concludes thus: "Ye are built upon the foundation of the apostles and prophets, Jesus Christ Himself being the chief corner-stone; in Whom all the building fitly framed together groweth unto an holy temple in the Lord: in Whom ye also are

[1] Eph. iii. 17. [2] Col. ii. 6, 7. [3] See Col. i. 23.

builded together for an habitation of God through the Spirit."[1] Now, all I will observe on this quotation is this: that I do not believe that the apostles and prophets are the foundation of which St. Paul speaks; but that Jesus Christ is foundation-stone and corner-stone in one. I would render it thus: "Built on the apostolic and prophetic foundation-stone" — the stone which apostles and prophets laid, and on which they themselves rest, — for "other foundation can no man lay, than that is laid," — namely, Christ. The other passage is in the Second Epistle to Timothy. Having spoken of the overthrowing of the faith of some, the Apostle adds: "Nevertheless, the foundation of God standeth sure, having this seal, The Lord knoweth them that are his: and, Let every one that nameth the name of Christ depart from iniquity."[2] What two grand inscriptions! Two eternal principles, one expressing the immutability of God, to drive away despair; the other describing the character of God's people, to drive away presumption. Well may they be indelibly cut on the apostolic and prophetic foundation.[3]

I said I would pass from the foundation to the step. The text to which I refer is again in one of the Pastoral Epistles: "They that have used the office of a deacon well purchase to themselves a good degree."[4] This is an interesting passage, and I hardly think it is to be understood as it is commonly

[1] Eph. ii. 20–22.
[2] 2 Tim. ii. 19.
[3] See Rev. xxi. 14.
[4] 1 Tim. iii. 13.

explained. The English word "*degree*" is correctly used in the sense of *a step for further progress*, as it is used in Shakespeare's "Julius Cæsar" of the climber up ambition's ladder: —

> "But when he once attains the utmost round,
> He then unto the ladder turns his back,
> Looks in the clouds, scorning *the base degrees*
> By which he did ascend."

I do not say that the words just quoted from St. Paul are generally interpreted in the spirit of this speech of Brutus; but the popular interpretation involves some risk of taking this direction. I cannot but hesitate to believe that St. Paul urges deacons to a discharge of duty either by the prospect of promotion, or by the charm of a higher position in the esteem of men. I should rather suppose that he alludes to their making sure of a firm spiritual standing, as before God and in prospect of the great day. This is more in harmony with the context. The "good degree" is coupled with "great boldness in the faith." All this they secure "to themselves." Besides doing service to the Church, they advance more and more in the confidence of their own spiritual life. With this expression it may be useful to compare what is said at the end of this Epistle (though there perhaps the metaphor is mixed), of the "laying up in store for ourselves a good foundation against the time to come, that we may lay hold on eternal life." [1] And it is certainly a coincidence of

[1] Tim. vi. 19.

some interest that all the passages which I have just been adducing in reference to the foundation and basement of buildings, are from Epistles addressed to Ephesus, where that celebrated Temple was, on the substructions of which immense labor and expense had been lavished, — that Temple which was full in sight when the mob cried out for two hours, "Great is Diana of the Ephesians."

But let us enter the house under the Apostle's guidance, and see what spiritual application he makes of the *furniture* which we find there. I follow the context of a passage which has already been partially quoted. In the Second Epistle to Timothy, in the second chapter, having described the foundation, he passes on to say: "But in a great house there are not only vessels of gold and of silver, but also of wood and of earth; and some to honor and some to dishonor. If a man therefore purge himself from these, he shall be a vessel unto honor, sanctified, and meet for the Master's use, and prepared unto every good work."[1] In the nineteenth verse he seems to set before us the Church in its essential character, as resting on an exclusive basis and marked by eternal principles; here, in what follows, the Church is exhibited to us in its mixed and outward character, lest erroneous conclusions should be drawn from the preceding. We have here a parable like the parable of the net; but we have something more than in the parable of the net. Not only are there two classes,

[1] 2 Tim. ii. 20, 21.

— vessels of rich material to honor, and vessels of mean material to dishonor, — but there are gradations in each class; gold and silver in the one, wood and earth in the other; not all among the good equally good, not all among the bad equally bad. A great house has a vast variety of furniture. In the twentieth verse we have the duty and the responsibility which arise from the consideration of this fact.

Our thoughts are carried, by natural association, from this passage to another of still more solemn import, where the same imagery is employed. I mean those verses in the ninth of the Romans, avowedly difficult even to the sternest Predestinarian, where the vessels of wrath are contrasted with the vessels of mercy: the former fitted (not by God) to destruction, the latter expressly prepared (by God) unto glory.[1] I think we gain something, in the exposition of this passage, by following the line of St. Paul's metaphorical language, and by putting the words in the Romans side by side with the other more explicit words addressed to Timothy. In that place we see that the Apostle does not urge his illustration beyond the point of contrast and classification. He does not say that because the furniture in a great house is separated into great classes, with subordinate gradations in each, therefore the members of the Church on earth are irrevocably so divided. He adds, that if a man keeps himself clear from association with the meaner vessels, he will himself become

[1] Rom. ix. 21–23.

one of the nobler. So in the Romans we have the two classes set before us: the sure tendency of the one to destruction, unless there is a recovery; the great truth that the glorious condition of the other is due to God only. All else is left open and untouched. The language is not so much argumentative as illustrative. It is of great importance, in the interpretation of Scripture, not to press a metaphor beyond the point which it was intended to elucidate, and not to deal with allegory as though it were logic.

Now, in drawing toward the conclusion of this section, I wish to revert to a remark which I made at the outset, namely, that a careful notice of the significance of imagery is all the more incumbent on us, in proportion as the circumstances from which that imagery is drawn may be peculiar. We ought to keep in mind the distinctive character of Classical Architecture, and to remember that it was from *this* architecture that St. Paul drew his illustrations. We are apt to give too Oriental a coloring to the New Testament, and this for an obvious reason. The Classical world has passed away. We must reproduce it, if we wish to see it as it was. But, to realize the outward circumstances of the Old Testament, we need only read the books of travellers, and study the pictures of modern artists. We see Abraham in every sheik; Rebecca is at the well near every village; the climate and the seasons are in the main unaltered. But the colonial lictors at Philippi, the Prætorium at Rome, Pilate with his official chair on the piece of tesselated pavement, — these must be reinstated in the scene, if we are to see them at all. The materials for reproducing the life exist in abundance in literature and museums, but the life itself does not exist; and the work of reproducing it requires the union of exact scholarship rightly applied, with a lively imagination under the control of judgment. Now, the illustrations which St. Paul connects with human habitations are not drawn from the wilderness, not from the transient dwellings of nomadic life, but from the solid cities of the Greeks and Romans. We might quote, in elucidation of this, a verse where he uses that very contrast to heighten the emphasis which he wishes to give to a forcible passage: "I know that if this earthly dwelling, which is only a tent, is taken to pieces, I have a *building* of God, a house not made with hands, eternal in the heavens." [1] Nor is it from any Eastern kind of architecture, but from Classical Architecture, that St. Paul draws his metaphors of this class. There is one passage which might at first sight be thought an exception; but it is not really such. I allude to that place in the Ephesians where he says that Christ has "broken down the middle wall of partition, that He might reconcile both Jews and Gentiles unto God in one body." [2] I imagine there is a tacit reference to that partition wall in the Jewish Temple, on which notices were put up, forbidding Gentiles to enter the

[1] 2 Cor. v. 1. [2] Eph. ii. 14, 16.

inner court. But then Herod's Temple was of Classical Architecture, like the great structures in Athens and Ephesus, not, as Solomon's may have been, of some Eastern Phœnician style, like the buildings of Tyre. Josephus gives us a full description of the Corinthian columns. Even the notices on the partition wall were in Latin and Greek. The complexion of Palestine in St. Paul's day was probably European rather than Asiatic; and we should be quite in error if we were to imagine the monotony of a modern Eastern town to be the type of what he habitually saw in Cæsarea, or even in Jerusalem.

Now, are there any peculiarities of Classical Architecture which we ought to take into account when we comment on any of the illustrations which, for our instruction, St. Paul was inspired to draw from that source? It seems to me that there are two. One is this, that all conspicuous Greek buildings, and most of the conspicuous Roman buildings, of his time, were characterized by vertical columns, supporting a horizontal entablature.

The significant application of this peculiarity is seen at once in that passage, where, in a time of controversy, he adduces the support of James and Cephas and John, who had the recognized reputation of being "pillars" in the Church.[1] Here the Church is evidently treated as a building, — a palace, or temple, or the like; and these three men are spoken of, not simply as stones in the building, just as ordinary

[1] Gal. ii. 9.

Christians might be, but as characteristic and essential parts, as both ornaments and supports.[1] Now, apply this to another context, concerning which some dispute has almost always existed: "These things I write, that thou mayest know how thou oughtest to behave thyself in the house of God, which is the Church of the living God, the pillar and ground of the truth."[2] I hold it to be an indefensible distortion of the passage, from polemical reasons, to take these last words and connect them with what follows, thus: "The pillar and ground of the truth, and without controversy great, is the mystery of godliness." I see no reason why the Church should not be called a pillar and support of the truth. What, indeed, would become of the light without the candlestick? But I am very much disposed, notwithstanding, to think that this is not the meaning of the passage. I am inclined to believe that Paul says this to Timothy: "I write to thee, seeing that thou hast a prominent and responsible place in the house of God, in order that thou mayest fill that place aright, and be thyself indeed a pillar and support of the truth." In favor of this view, we have the analogy of the passage just adduced from the Galatians. We have also this consideration, that the Church is a building, not a pillar, while a pillar is a partial support of a classical building, and one ornament out of many. It is in the criticism of just such a passage as this that I would claim for Archæology its right to be combined with Philology.

1 See Rev. iii. 12. 2 1 Tim. iii. 14, 15.

Not that there is any grammatical objection to the interpretation I am advocating; nor is the sanction wanting of early commentators, whose instinctive sense in a case of this kind is of considerable moment.

The other architectural feature of ancient cities, to which I desire to invite attention, brings us at once to the passage from that third chapter of the First Epistle to the Corinthians, to which reference was made at the outset. I believe that in such cities as Ephesus, where the letter was written, or Corinth, to which it was addressed, there was a signal difference (far greater than in modern European cities) between the gorgeous splendor of the great public buildings, and the meanness and squalor of those streets where the poor and profligate resided. The former were constructed of marble and granite; the capitals of their columns and their roofs were richly decorated with silver and gold; the latter were mean structures, run up with boards for walls, with straw in the interstices, and thatch on the top. This is the contrast on which St. Paul seizes — slabs and pillars of marble and granite, and gold and silver, on one hand; wood, hay, stubble, on the other, — to set forth two very different results of the spiritual edification (I use the word in its neutral sense) which goes on in the Church. Sometimes the passage is treated as though the picture presented were that of a dunghill of straw and sticks, with jewels, such as diamonds and emeralds, among the rubbish. But such an image would be utterly improbable in itself, and out of harmony with all the context. The whole allegory is strictly and consistently architectural.[1]

In order to enter into the full significance of the allegory, we should look at the context. St. Paul is addressing those who were addicted to the spirit of party, and is speaking of the right estimate of Christian ministers. He first uses an agricultural metaphor, and then he passes to an architectural. Our approach to the architectural structure lies, as it were, through a garden or orchard. Here Paul has planted the precious trees. Apollos, and probably others with him, as subordinates and successors to Paul, are watering them. Suddenly the image changes to a new one, more capable of being turned to what the Apostle wishes to enforce. A building in progress rises before us. Paul has laid the foundation, — laid it once for all, and laid it well. He has no objection to say this, for it has been done by the grace of God. On this foundation Apollos and others are building. As to building on another foundation, this is set aside at once. The work is going on, and will go on indefinitely in the future; but it will be tested. A day will come when the fire will burn up those wretched edifices of wood and straw, and leave unharmed in their glorious beauty those that were raised of marble and granite, and decorated with silver and gold. The men who raised such structures as these shall not only be safe, but rewarded; the men who lost their time on the others shall just escape out of the confla-

[1] See pp. 126–129.

gration, because they built on the right foundation, but their escape shall be barely an escape.

It is a most serious admonition to the minister of the Gospel "to take heed how he buildeth," that is, with what materials,—what kind of teaching, what kind of parochial arrangements, what kind of provision for the young, what kind of care for tender consciences or for desperate guilt. He should consider, too, what his materials have cost him. If they are cheap and worthless, the first that came to hand, what fate can he expect for his building in the day of trial? Is it not well worth his while to see that the quarry is worked for the stone, and the mine explored deep for the silver and the gold, that all his materials may be precious, solid, and good, and may survive the fire, as the temples of Corinth itself survived the conflagration of Mummius, which burnt the hovels around?

It will be gathered that I think the building itself in this passage is not simply the development of doctrine and the promotion of sound practical truth. These I look on as the materials of building. The building itself I should regard, in analogy with all that has preceded, as the *persons*, or rather I ought to say the *characters*, which result from this good or bad edification.

But still the passage may be lawfully applied to remind us of the importance of regular and systematic instruction in religious truth. And hence a lesson may be drawn, which has reference to the responsibility of the recipients, not the givers, of instruction. And we may conclude with an extract from the first of the Catechetical Lectures of St. Cyril, which he delivered about the year 347 A. D. in the grand Basilica erected by Constantine the Great: "Abide thou in the catechisings," he says. "Though our discourse be long, let not thy mind be wearied out For thou art receiving thine armor against the antagonist power: against heresies, against Jews, and Samaritans, and Gentiles. Thou hast many enemies. Take to thee many darts." He uses here the military imagery, which was the subject of the first of these essays. Presently he uses the agricultural imagery, which will be the subject of the next of the series. "Study the things that are spoken, and keep them forever, — considering this to be the planting season. Unless we dig, and that deeply, how shall that afterwards be planted rightly which has once been planted ill?" And then — quite in St. Paul's own manner — he passes to the simile with the consideration of which we have been occupied in the present essay, — "Or consider catechising to be a kind of building. Unless we dig deep, and lay the foundation; unless by successive fastenings in the masonry we bind the framework of the house together, that no opening be detected, nor the work be left unsound, nought avails all our former labor. But stone must succeed stone in course, and corner must follow corner, and, inequalities being smoothed away, the masonry must rise regular. In like manner, we are bringing to thee stones, as it were, of knowledge. Thou must hear concerning the living God; concerning the Judgment; concerning Christ; concerning the Resurrection; and many things are made to follow one the other, which, though now dropped one by one, at length are presented in harmonious connection. But if thou wilt not connect them into one whole, and remember what is first, and what is second, the builder indeed buildeth, but the building will be unstable."

III.

ANCIENT AGRICULTURE.

RAPID transitions from one metaphor to another are characteristic of St. Paul.

One transition of this kind is to be found in the eighth verse of the tenth chapter of the Second Epistle to the Corinthians. St. Paul has been using language drawn from the incidents of a campaign to describe the course which he himself might be forced to adopt, if those to whom he writes, or others, were to persist in their disobedience. In such a case he might be compelled to put all his spiritual power into action, and to "pull down" their "strongholds" of arrogance and pride, just as the rock-forts of his native Cilicia were destroyed in the Roman wars with the pirates. Such a course of procedure would be a cause of deep regret to him; for, as he says in the verse before us, "the authority" which "the Lord had given," was intended for purposes of "edification," or building up, not for purposes of "destruction," or pulling down. This is the last echo of the military image, — or rather not the very last echo, for the identical phrase is found again at the very close of the Epistle,[1] — but it *is* an echo of the mil-

[1] See 2 Cor. xiii. 10.

itary image, though in the English version it is muffled, as it were, so as to be almost inaudible; and the fact to which attention is invited is the close juxtaposition in one sentence of the military and the architectural metaphor.

Another instance of rapid transition may introduce us directly to the subject of the present section. The *agricultural* metaphors of St. Paul are not by any means the most prominent, but they constitute a sufficient topic for one essay. "Ye are God's husbandry, ye are God's building," he says to the Corinthians, in the ninth verse of the third chapter of his First Epistle. The agricultural and the architectural image are here side by side, as, in the last case, the architectural and the military. We have already given our attention to the architectural allegory which follows this point of transition. Our subject now is the agricultural allegory which precedes it: "I have planted, Apollos watered; but God gave the increase. So then neither is he that planteth anything, neither he that watereth: but God that giveth the increase. Now he that planteth and he that watereth are one; and every man shall receive his own reward according to his own labor. For we are laborers together with God: ye are God's husbandry." [1]

Paley points out very acutely the delicate yet perfectly unconscious harmony of this passage with what we read in the Acts, and uses it as an argument for the authenticity of both the Epistle and the History.

[1] 1 Cor. iii. 6–9.

Not only must Paul have been at Corinth before Apollos, but Apollos must have been there in the interval between the Apostle's visit and the writing of this letter. This is not our subject now, except so far as this, that it leads us to mark more closely the Providential sequence of one teacher after another in God's gracious work of preparing and maturing his Church.

This image of a large cultivated garden, in which many are employed, is indeed a most apt, a most copious illustration of nearly all the main characteristics of the Christian Ministry. There is first the succession of which I have spoken, the tasks assigned now to one and now to another, according to the law of the seasons and the will of the great Master of the garden, one beginning when another has left off; one completing what another has prepared. At the same time there is justice to each: "Every man shall receive his own reward according to his own labor." And yet all the work is one. Though many hands are employed, according to their aptitude and the time when they are required, the progress is one through the advancing year to one result: "He that planteth and he that watereth are one." All, too, is entirely dependent on an unseen power: "Neither is he that planteth anything, neither he that watereth: but God that giveth the increase." Then there are the lessons of cheerfulness, hopefulness, and patience; the habit of not looking for immediate results, but at the same time the confident expectation that in spite of adverse weather the flower and fruit will come at last, which all are necessarily associated with the very thought of a garden, and which should be diligently fostered by every Christian minister in his own heart and mind. And lastly, there is the duty of giving diligent heed to the young plants. How much may be expected, if they are vigilantly and carefully tended at first, one by one! "Let us get up early to the vineyards; let us see if the vine flourish, whether the tender grape appear, and the pomegranates bud forth."[1]

It has been said before, that the references to nature in St. Paul's writings are almost entirely to nature in connection with human labor; not to its beauty and to the impressions which the mind passively receives from it, but to its useful and beneficent processes under the work of cultivation. There is hardly any mere natural imagery in his Epistles. We find more of this kind of illustration in the one short Epistle of St. James, than in all the writings of St. Paul. What we read in the fifteenth chapter of the first letter to the Corinthians, — "There is one glory of the sun, and another glory of the moon, and another glory of the stars: for one star differeth from another star in glory,"[2] — is no real exception to this. This is not an outburst of adoring admiration, like those of the Psalmist "when he considered the heavens, the work of God's fingers, the moon and the stars, which He had ordained."[3] It is really

[1] Cant. vii. 12. [2] 1 Cor. xv. 41. [3] Ps. viii. 3.

the continuance of the preceding argument, and a new illustration arising out of that which he had used before. He had been speaking of the difference between "bodies terrestrial," or the organization of beings like ourselves adapted to an existence on earth; and "bodies celestial," or the organization of beings like the angels, adapted to a heavenly residence. And nothing is more natural (if I may so speak) than that this contrast should suggest another connected with the heavens themselves. The sun, the moon, and the stars, though they all give light, are very different among themselves, and each is suited to its own place and its own function. So above he had said that among the organisms of animal life on the earth there are great varieties, each according to its office in the economy of God's world: "All flesh is not the same flesh; but there is one kind of flesh of men, another flesh of beasts, another of fishes, and another of birds." Now, going backwards again along the line of the Apostle's illustrations, we have the passage which I am aiming at: "But some man will say, How are the dead raised up? and with what body do they come? Thou fool, that which thou sowest is not quickened except it die: and that which thou sowest, thou sowest not that body that shall be, but bare grain, it may chance of wheat, or of some other grain: but God giveth it a body as it hath pleased Him, and to every seed his own body."[1] Here we have that reference to nature

[1] 1 Cor. xv. 35-38.

in its connection with human labor and its productive operations rather than its mere phenomena, to which allusion was made just now. As, in speaking to the uneducated Lystrians, St. Paul had urged "the rains from heaven and the fruitful seasons" as an argument for gratitude and a lesson against idolatry, so here he presses on the speculative Corinthians the facts with which they were familiar in the sowing and reaping of every year, as one reason for casting aside all theoretical objections to a resurrection of the body. The grain and the corn-plant, the seed and the harvest, are the same, and yet not the same. They are so connected as to be identical, and yet a wonderful change of form and organization has taken place under the operation of mysterious laws. Why should it be otherwise with our own frames? He returns to this illustration again, after deviating just rapidly to touch the other illustrations: "So also is the resurrection of the dead. It is sown in corruption, it is raised in incorruption; it is sown in dishonor, it is raised in glory; it is sown in weakness, it is raised in power; it is sown a natural body, it is raised a spiritual body. There is a natural body, and there is a spiritual body."[1] We have here, then, what I think may truly be termed an agricultural allegory. The appeal is to the universal experience of man in the work of husbandry. And if there is just one Jewish touch where the subject is first approached in this chapter, — "Christ the first-fruits, afterwards they

[1] 1 Cor. xv. 42-44.

that are Christ's at his coming," — this is quite what we should expect.[1]

This image of the harvest, in various applications, as we know, pervades the whole of Scripture from its very earliest portions, from the dreams of Joseph or of Pharaoh, and the gleaning of Ruth and her mother. But St. Paul uses it so pointedly, and so much in a way of his own, that I think it may be included as an element in his characteristic style. The progressive change of organization, along with absolute identity of being, has just been adduced as a type of the Resurrection. How solemnly is this thought (in the sixth chapter of the Galatians) connected with the ultimate results to ourselves in eternity of the life which we lead in the moments of our time! "Be not deceived; God is not mocked; for whatsoever a man soweth, that shall he also reap. For he that soweth to his flesh shall of the flesh reap corruption; but he that soweth to the Spirit shall of the Spirit reap life everlasting."[2] Here is the principle of inevitable retribution, the growing and growing, according to irresistible laws; the moral organism passing into new forms without losing its identity, just as the rich waving harvest is developed from the poor shriveled grain. And clearly here the human side of the subject, the actual agricultural process, is a very prominent part of the image and the lesson, whether it be viewed in the aspect of warning or of encouragement. And the same train of thought meets

[1] Cor. xv. 20, 23.

[2] Gal. vi. 7, 8.

us in a nearly contemporary Epistle, in reference to another subject, namely, the blessing, "twice blest," of generous giving: "He which soweth sparingly shall reap also sparingly; and he which soweth bountifully shall reap also bountifully;" "God loveth a cheerful giver." It is written of such a man that he "disperses abroad; he gives to the poor;" and yet he is no loser; his "righteousness" — or rather it ought to be, his liberality and beneficence, his power of doing good — "endureth" still.[1] A man is no loser by sowing his grain, in faith, with an open hand; he secures the harvest, and he secures a larger supply of grain than ever, for sowing in future over wider fields. In the encouraging verses which conclude the passage, I will not stay to inquire whether the true reading gives the Apostle's words in the form of a promise or a prayer; for indeed promises and prayers in the Apostolic writings run into one another, so that we can hardly distinguish them, even as the readings of the manuscripts do in such passages. "Now He that ministereth seed to the sower," in the world of nature and in the work of agriculture, "may He multiply (or, He shall multiply) your seed sown, and increase the fruits of your righteousness," — or rather, as before, "your liberality and beneficence," — "being enriched in everything unto all bountifulness, which causeth through us thanksgiving to God."[1] No imagery could set before us more vividly the rich and increasing reward which waits upon

[1] 2 Cor. ix. 6-9. [2] 2 Cor. ix. 10, 11.

faithful and generous service on our side, or the overflowing blessing on God's side, which gives life and abundance and growth to all honest spiritual husbandry.

This passage leads me to single out a word which is certainly very characteristic of St. Paul. The word "*riches*" has often been noticed as marking his style; and the same is true of the word "*fruit;*" and not merely is this a verbal, but also a moral characteristic. It seems to me to express that kind of exuberance, so to speak, which will never allow him to hope and believe by halves. The former word is a metaphor from the market, the latter from the corn-field or the orchard. He desires to visit the Romans, that he may "have some *fruit* among them also, as among other Gentiles." [1] Writing to the Philippians of the precariousness of his life, he says (so I understand him), that he valued this continuance "in the flesh" as the condition of bringing forth "*fruit*" in his work.[2] Writing to the Colossians, his expression concerning the Gospel is, that in all the world it is ever "growing," and ever "bringing forth *fruit*."[3] And this I notice (unless I am mistaken) as a mark of St. Paul's way of using this word, that he always applies it to what is *good*. And that this should be so seems to us very appropriate and very beautiful. The blessedness of the righteous man is that, planted as he is "by the water side," he "bringeth forth his fruit in due season," whereas

[1] Rom. i. 13. [2] Phil. i. 22. [3] Col. i. 6.

the ungodly is "like the chaff which the wind driveth away."[1] The passage which most naturally occurs to us here is that in the Galatians, where the *fruit* of the Spirit is contrasted in detail with the *works* of the flesh.[2] It is a contrast very similar to that which we find elsewhere between the *wages* of sin and the *gift* of God.[3] Nor is that passage in the Galatians a solitary instance. We find the same in the Ephesians, — "Walk as children of the light; for the *fruit* of light is in all goodness and righteousness and truth,"[4] the force of which is very much enhanced by our observing what follows: "Have no fellowship with the *unfruitful* works of darkness." And similar language is found in the Epistle to the Romans, — "What *fruit* had ye then in those things whereof ye are now ashamed?" but "now, being emancipated" from that dreadful master, sin, and "become servants to God, ye have your *fruit* unto holiness, and the end everlasting life."[5] Sometimes the phrase is applied generally, as (not to repeat again that passage concerning "the *fruits* of righteousness" addressed to the Corinthians)[6] when he desires that the Philippians may be "filled" with those "*fruits* of righteousness which are by Jesus Christ to the glory and praise of God,"[7] or that the Colossians may be "*fruitful* in every good work, and increase in the knowledge of God."[8] Sometimes

1 Ps. i. 3, 4. 2 Gal. v. 19–23. 3 See Rom. vi. 23.
4 Eph. v. 8, 9, 11. 5 Rom. vi. 21, 22. 6 2 Cor. ix. 10.
7 Phil. i. 11. 8 Col. i. 10.

the reference is specific, as when he says that he is going to Jerusalem to deliver and lay up safely in store, and to seal, "the *fruit*" of the liberality of the Christians in Macedonia and Achaia; [1] or when he says afterwards of similar generosity which came to himself from Macedonia, "Not because I desire a gift, but I desire *fruit* that may abound to your account;" [2] or when he urges in one of the Pastoral Epistles, that they who profess Christ's religion must learn to maintain good works, and contribute to those wants of others which must of necessity be brought before them, in order that with all this profession they "be not *unfruitful*." [3] But in all these cases, whether they are general or specific, the reference is to what is good. One apparent exception may very naturally here come into the mind, namely, that passage in which two consecutive verses end, the former with the phrase "bring forth *fruit* unto God," the latter with the phrase, "bring forth *fruit* unto death." [4] But these verses occur in the seventh of the Romans, and even if the image were the same, I think it would be natural to call the passage an oxymoron, and so it would really be an instance of the rule, and not an exception. I conceive, however, that the image is different, and that the reference is to fruit as the offspring of marriage. I believe it will be found true, that when St. Paul applies to moral subjects the word "fruit," as derived from the corn-field or

1 Rom. xv. 28.
2 Phil. iv. 17.
3 Tit. iii. 14.
4 Rom. vii. 4, 5.

the orchard, he applies it to what is good. I say nothing of the other parts of Scripture. But it is as if he thought the term too honorable — expressing as it does the result of man's honest, useful labor, in subordination to and in dependence on the bounteous and life-giving influences of Heaven, — too honorable and too cheerful to be applied to what is bad. "The root of the righteous yieldeth fruit."[1] "He shall be as a tree planted by the waters, neither shall cease from yielding fruit."[2]

One particular passage — a remarkable and difficult passage — in that Epistle to the Romans, now claims a moment of close attention.[3] I allude, of course, to the allegory drawn in the eleventh chapter from the grafting of the olive-tree. The image first appears in the sixteenth verse, and (as we have seen in other instances) in close combination with another image, — "If the first-fruit be holy, the lump is also holy; and if the root be holy, so are the branches;" and then it is rapidly developed with varied and pointed application up to the end of the twenty-fourth verse. With all the great doctrinal and historical questions arising from this passage, we have on the present occasion nothing to do; our concern is with the outward imagery, and in it there is this very strange circumstance, that the lesson is drawn from the grafting of branches of a wild olive-tree on the stock of a good olive-tree — the grafting of branches of a wild fruit-tree on the stock of a good fruit-tree,

[1] Prov. xii. 12. [2] Jer. xvii. 8. [3] Rom. xi. 16–24.

— a process unheard of among gardeners. Commentators have tortured themselves with this difficulty, and some of them have adduced instances of this process with certain supposed good results as regards the productiveness of the olive. I confess I am very skeptical on this point, and the explanation which I suggest is very simple, though I am not aware of having seen it previously suggested elsewhere. I believe that here partly is the very point of the parable, that the grafting *was* contrary to the law of nature. So strange a grafting as that which had taken place in the case of the Gentiles made the lesson far more emphatic to them. It was the very *contrary* to the grafting which took place in the olive-grounds to which all readers of the Epistle were accustomed. This work of artificial cultivation is indeed the basis of the parable, but it is the basis by way of contrast rather than of comparison. So our Lord, in St. Luke's Gospel, compares God to a *selfish* man and an *unjust* judge, and makes the argument for the answering of prayer all the stronger.[1] Or let us take another illustration. St. James says to the rich tyrants of his day, "Your gold and silver is rusted, and the rust of them shall be a witness against you." [2] Now gold does not rust. St. James was quite aware of this. But herein, I apprehend, is one part of the point of the image. Their very gold should become mysteriously their curse. So in the case before us. St. Paul knew very well the pro-

[1] See Luke xi. 8; xviii. 6. [2] James v. 3.

cesses which took place in the olive-grounds which were abundant then, as they are now, in all parts of the Levant. He must have seen them often when he was a boy at Tarsus. Boys notice all such things; and the experience of early life becomes, even in an Apostle, the basis of religious teaching. To find fault with him for inexactness, seems to me very like finding fault with him (as some critics do in these days) for inaccurate applications of the Old Testament. He knew the Old Testament, and so did his Jewish readers, far better than we do. But we must not leave our proper subject.

And one other side of the subject must be touched before it has been handled completely. Agriculture has to do with the animal as well as the vegetable world; and something within this province, too, in the writings of St. Paul, will reward our careful attention.

I have sometimes been impressed with the fact, while thinking of this topic, that the critical words addressed to the Apostle from heaven at the threshold of his Christian career, were in truth *an agricultural metaphor*, "Saul! Saul! it is hard for thee" — Who knows — I write it with reverence — whether at that moment the operations of ploughing might not be going on within sight of the road along which the persecutor was travelling? At all events, the image is certainly drawn from those operations, as certainly as the images in the Sermon on the Mount were drawn from the lilies which grew in the field, or the birds which flew over it. All who have journeyed in the East, or even in the South of Europe, are familiar with that ox-goad, the resistance to which only increases the suffering of the restive animal, and in allusion to which the force of conscience, sharpened by God's Spirit, is depicted in the words, "It is hard for thee to kick against the pricks."[1] And it seems to me interesting to notice, on the one hand, that our blessed Lord's words, spoken on this occasion from heaven, were a parable, like the parables which He graciously uttered on earth, and, on the other hand, that they are in harmony with, and might almost be fancied to have given a holy suggestion of, one class of the Apostle's own habitual imagery.

I may remark that what was said in the earlier part of this section in reference to orchards, vineyards, and corn-fields, has its counterpart here in reference to flocks and oxen. St. Paul's illustrative language deals with human labor and its useful results, rather than with nature viewed poetically on the side of beauty and mere expressiveness. Accordingly, the animals under the care of man are presented to us more on the industrial side than the contemplative. It is the farmer near the large town, rather than the shepherd in the wilderness, who comes before us in the pages of this Apostle. It is remarkable that nowhere, in all his unquestioned Epistles,[2] is Jesus Christ set forth as the Good Shepherd. I do not forget those touching words in the address at Miletus, "Take

[1] Acts xxvi. 14. [2] See Heb. xiii. 20.

heed to the flock; feed the Church which God hath purchased with his own blood; for grievous wolves shall enter in, not sparing the flock."[1] And perhaps it would be strange if no one instance were found in St. Paul of the employment of an image which is almost universal throughout the rest of Scripture. But still it is not characteristic of his style. It is very different with regard to St. Peter, in whose First Epistle these words, "Feed the flock; be examples to the flock,"[2] are a true echo of the words at the end of the Gospels, "Feed my sheep, feed my lambs."[3]

With St. Paul's habit of illustration the concourse of men, where business goes on and buying and selling, is more in harmony than the solitary mountain-side, where the sheep are following their shepherd and diligently cropping the thin herbage on the rocky slopes. We see this in that passage of his Epistles when he does mention the *flock*, "Who goeth a warfare any time at his own charges? Who planteth a vineyard, and eateth not of the fruit thereof? or who feedeth a flock, and eateth not of the milk of the flock?"[4] the real meaning of which is this, "Who keeps a vineyard or a flock of sheep without living by the profits of the grapes and the milk, when they are brought into the market?" In this case, as in so many others, three metaphors — one military and two agricultural — are rapidly thrown together. The

1 Acts xx. 28, 29.
2 1 Pet. v. 2, 3.
3 John xxi. 15-17.
4 1 Cor. ix. 7.

point on which they are brought to bear is the claim which Christian ministers have on the support of the people, whether or not they may find it necessary or politic to urge that claim. With this it seems natural to combine another passage in another Epistle (remarkable also for the heaping up of metaphors), though there the duty of the *minister* to *labor* among his people is urged, his support being assumed, while here it is *their* duty to *support* him which is pressed, his labor being assumed. "No man that enters on a soldier's career mixes himself up with the common business of life; no man, striving in the games will obtain the prize unless he has kept the rules; the husbandman that laboreth must be first partaker of the fruits;"[1] *i. e.*, it is the farmer that works who has *the first claim* to the profits of the produce of the farm. The idle farmer, the idle clergyman, deserves to starve. Perhaps the word "fruits" might more naturally seem to connect this sentence with the earlier part of this section; but it is better to have taken it in its present connection, because of the common bearing of both these passages on one subject — the Christian ministry — which also is the subject of the one remaining passage with which I am now about to conclude.

"Thou shalt not muzzle the mouth of the ox that treadeth out the corn." When a sentence from the Old Testament is more than once quoted in the New Testament, it always seems to have a peculiar claim

[1] 2 Tim. ii. 4–6.

on our reverent attention. And St. Paul quotes this sentence from Deuteronomy[1] twice, in two Epistles written at very different periods, and each time brings it to bear on the same topic. "It is written in the law of Moses, Thou shalt not muzzle the mouth of the ox that treadeth out the corn. Doth God take care for oxen? or saith He it altogether for our sakes? For our sakes, no doubt, this is written: that he that plougheth should plough in the hope of a harvest, and he that thresheth should do this in the hope of partaking of the harvest"[2] (for so I conceive the true meaning of the latter words would be given). The eye ranges here over the whole agricultural process, from the ploughing and sowing to the reaping and threshing, and all this ought to be conducted in hope; otherwise all the cheerfulness, all the elasticity of the work is gone. The Christian people ought to be very careful that their clergy are not weighed down by the perpetual harassing care of the maintenance of their families and the education of their children. When they see all the harvest of wealth around them, they ought, if they labor patiently, at least to have some small share of it. There may possibly, as Chrysostom says, be a hint to them, — to this effect, that they do labor diligently, that they be not impatient under the irksome monotony of routine, and that they be content with, it may be, a very scanty portion of all this profusion of wealth. But the main lesson is to the Christian people, that they support

[1] Deut. xxv. 4.

[2] 1 Cor. ix. 9, 10.

the hearts and the strength of their clergy by endowments, and gifts, and liberal payments, and still more by sympathy, and respect, and large coöperation. The lesson is riveted forever on the Church, in strong words, by the other passage, "Let the elders that rule well be counted worthy of double honor, especially they who labor in the word and doctrine; for the Scripture saith, Thou shalt not muzzle the ox that treadeth out the corn."[1] How beautifully is this large lesson of charity and justice developed out of what might seem a very trivial and unimportant precept! "Doth God take care for oxen?" Certainly He does, but He takes care for man much more. When He tells us that it is a duty to be considerate of the former, He reminds us that it is a still more urgent duty to feel sympathy for the latter. It is our Lord's argument, "Not a sparrow falls to the ground without your Father: ye are of more value than many sparrows;"[2] and again, "Which of you shall have a sheep fallen into a pit on the Sabbath and will not lift it out? How much is a man better than a sheep?"[3] By thus inculcating the duty of considerately caring for dumb animals, the Jewish Law really enforces the general principle, the wider duty, which embraces all things, "both great and small." Our poet's words come here irresistibly into the mind, —

> "The dear God who loveth us
> He made and loveth all."

And indeed this considerate care in the minor instance

[1] 1 Tim. v. 17, 18. [2] Matt. x. 29, 31. [3] Matt. xii. 11, 12.

is itself a training for humanity and kindness in reference to the greater. Such a suggestion as that of this little precept in the Pentateuch, furnished to a thoughtful, devout, and feeling mind, spreads out into a thousand instances, and finds its opportunities in all the relations of life, and especially those relations where service on our behalf has established a claim to our gratitude.

IV.

GREEK GAMES.

THE four short essays in which I am inviting attention to four of St. Paul's favorite metaphors, do not by any means exhaust the characteristic imagery of that Apostle; and in order to give a better completeness to the series, it may be useful to prefix to this last essay a few general remarks on the whole subject.

A single example, selected out of those which have previously been given, may (though at the risk of some repetition) conveniently introduce these general remarks. St. Paul, in writing his First Epistle to the Corinthians, says to them, as we have seen,[1] "Ye are God's building." These simple words are like the striking of a key-note. There follows immediately the full swell of a familiar passage,[2] with all its melodious rhythm, and its intricate verbal and moral harmonies. There is no need to occupy ourselves again with the religious meanings of the passage. Attention is simply directed to the characteristic nature of the allegory. If we place ourselves at Ephesus, where the letter was written, or at Corinth, where the letter was received, and mark the evident and

[1] See p. 40.

[2] 1 Cor. iii. 9-15.

outward characteristics of such places, we see at once the significance of the language. Conspicuous in these cities were vast public buildings, such as the Temple of Diana at Ephesus,[1] and similar edifices at Corinth; strong, firm, and magnificent, with columns and slabs of marble, porphyry, and granite — "precious stones — " and richly completed with metallic decorations, "gold and silver." But close beside them were the hovels of the poor, with a sharpness of contrast to which we are not accustomed, but which we can in some degree set before our minds by imagining some of our great public edifices to be densely surrounded by an accumulation of wretched villages, with huts hastily run up with "wood," the interstices filled with "hay," and the roof thatched with "stubble." And now suppose a fire to take place in such a scene, and you have immediately the simple outward image on which the Apostle's manifold parable rests. All these wretched hovels, so cheaply, so carelessly built, would be burnt up; and all that could be hoped for to the poor man himself, in any one of them, would be a bare personal escape through the flames. The great building, on the other hand, might be scorched and blackened, but it would stand steady and erect, and exhibit still all the proofs of patient working in the quarry, of good and solid masonry, and of rich and elaborate ornament. In listening to expositions of this passage, we often find that this plain and simple way of looking at it has never

[1] See Acts xix. 27.

occurred to the expositor, and we are presented with the unreal and grotesque image of a rubbish-heap, consisting of sticks and straw, and containing also some contents of a jeweler's shop, diamonds, rubies, and garnets. This is not the style in which St. Paul would be likely to write to educated men. And misconceptions of such a kind arise from this, that men, in interpreting Scripture, so often look only at the words and not at the things; so often forget that every writer in the Bible drew his illustrations from the circumstances with which he was surrounded, and especially those circumstances which were most in harmony with the temperament of mind which the Holy Ghost, in that particular case, consecrated and employed.

The general notion, then, of these essays is this, that in order to enter into the full force of St. Paul's writings it is needful to have, not only that clear apprehension of the meaning of his words, which we obtain through our exact study of Greek literature, but also that apprehension of the familiar sights and sounds, customs and institutions, surrounding him, which is furnished by our knowledge of history and antiquities, science and art; and further, to consider carefully what portions of that outward environment he most employs by preference or habit in the inculcation of religious truth. In studying the Bible, the dictionary of things is almost as important as the dictionary of words; and St. Paul's writings are no exception to this rule, but one of its best exemplifications.

As to his own temperament and predilection, we may again revert to a remark which was made before,[1] that his metaphors are usually drawn, not from the operations and phenomena of the natural world, but from the activities and the outward manifestations of human life. In this respect St. Paul's illustrative language has already been contrasted with that of St. James: "The vapor, the fierce wind, the fountain, beasts and birds and serpents, the flower of the grass, the wave of the sea, the early and latter rain, the sun risen with a burning heat,"[2] — these are like the figures of the ancient prophets. There is more imagery of this kind, I think, in the one short Epistle of St. James than in all the speeches and letters of St. Paul put together. The address to the idolaters of Lystra,[3] country people as they were in a rude and remote district, if it is an exception at all, is exactly that kind of exception which makes the general rule more palpably evident.

St. Paul's favorite figures are undoubtedly taken from the midst of the busiest human society. Four of these have been selected for careful examination, and we are now proceeding to consider the fourth. But others of the same general type might easily have been added to the list; and again, for the sake of completeness it may be desirable to name two or three instances. Thus, first, how large a portion of St. Paul's attention is given to *money-matters!* How

[1] Page 48. [2] James iv. 14; iii. 4, 7, 11, 12; i. 6, 10, 11; v. 7. [3] Acts xiv. 15–17.

often are his images drawn from the market! To take only three instances: "Owe no man anything, but to love one another."[1] It would be impossible, perhaps, by the use of any other illustration, to express with equal force all that this sentence implies. Again, in the phrase, "Redeem the time,"[2] what is really said is this, "Buy out of the market what you may never buy so cheap again; use the opportunity while you have it, and use it thoroughly." So again, his reference to the *law courts* and the administration of justice, even when he is arguing points of theology, is an instance which strikes us forcibly. An interesting question arises, whether in such passages he refers mainly to Jewish law or to Roman law, especially when the allusion is to marriage[3] and the making of wills;[4] but in either case his consistency is preserved as regards the characteristic nature of his imagery. A third instance is that of *slavery*, as was almost inevitable for such a writer at this period of history. In the ancient world, war and slavery ran into one another; and throughout the Roman empire the whole of society was made up of the contrasts of "bond" and "free,"[5] with the freedmen (and such, probably, were St. Paul's own ancestors) intermediate between the two. Hence, when speaking of the most momentous alternatives in the condition of the soul, his language is drawn

[1] Rom. xiii. 8.
[2] Eph. v. 16; Col. iv. 5.
[3] Rom. vii. 3, 4.
[4] Gal. iii. 15; iv. 1.
[5] 1 Cor. xii. 13; Gal. iii. 28; Col. iii. 11.

from the experience of slaves. The great and decisive change is expressed thus: "Being emancipated from that cruel master, Sin, ye are now the happy slaves of a good master, God.[1] But it is time to proceed without delay to our proper subject. The imagery to which our special consideration is to be given now is the most animated of all, being derived from the lively and exciting *games of the Greeks.*

There is an obvious reason why images of this kind should have been very familiar to St. Paul's thoughts, and why, when made the vehicles of instruction, they should have been very helpful to his converts. Wherever he was residing, at Corinth, at Athens, and in all places where a Greek population was predominant (and this was, in fact, over the whole of the Levant), the athletic games of the Greeks came before his notice, as a subject which caused the most engrossing and universal interest. The *Gymnasium,* or place of training, and the *Stadium,* or ground for running, were among the most conspicuous and most frequented spots in the architecture and embellishment of the cities. Of many of them the remains can still be traced. Wrestling, boxing, and especially foot-races, with all the preliminary training, with the assembled and applauding multitudes while the contest was going on, with the formality of the heralds and the strict observance of the rules, with the umpires and prizes and eager congratulations at the close, with the poems which perpetuated great victories like

1 Rom. vi. 18, 22. See vii. 23; viii. 21.

heir-looms through successive generations, — these things were almost a religion among the Greeks, and they caused an enthusiasm which we ourselves can hardly understand, though it does happen that in our day athletic sports are a fancy and a fashion, and really in some cases, it would seem, almost a religion.

I said, especially the foot-race. This was preëminently the struggle which caused the most eager interest in that age and in those countries. And this is preëminently the image which seems to come obviously to the Apostle, when he employs comparisons of this kind. We find instances in the Book of Acts. Thus when he is preaching one of his great missionary sermons at Antioch in Pisidia, and has occasion to mention John the Baptist, he speaks of him as "*fulfilling his course*,"[1] which literally means, "running the race he had to run;" and this lively expression is evidently a fitting representation of that career, which did not last very long, but was very energetic while it lasted. So in addressing the elders at Miletus, and speaking of himself, and alluding with deep feeling to the "bonds and afflictions" which awaited him, he says: "None of these things move me, neither count I my life dear unto myself, that I may *finish my course* with joy."[2] He knows that his course requires a vigorous effort; he feels that there are many things to dissuade him from it and to cause him to turn aside; but he braces himself up, like a runner, for the struggle, throws himself into it with

1 Acts xiii. 25. 2 Acts xx. 24.

all his force and spirit, and thinks of the joy and exultation which await him at the close.

Similar, and very frequently, is his language in the Epistles. It is well worth our while to observe how generally and variously this figure is distributed through them. Some phrases of this kind must appear strange to those who do not consider the context of circumstances by which the Apostle was surrounded. Thus, to take as our guide the same English word which we have observed in the Acts: "Pray for us," he says to the Thessalonians, "that the word of the Lord may have *free course* and be glorified."[1] Here the Gospel itself is the runner, for which he desires a race that shall be vigorous, rapid, free from obstacles, and triumphant at the end. Again, to turn to most pathetic language having reference to himself, he writes to Timothy, "I have fought the good fight; I have finished *my course;* I have kept the faith; henceforth there is laid up for me the crown of righteousness, which the Lord, the righteous Judge, shall give me at that day."[2] We must be careful here to give the right meaning to the word "fight." This term has nothing to do with war. It denotes an *athletic* contest. And the particular kind of athletic contest, which he specifies in his customary way, is the foot-race. But now he is writing near the close of life. The race is nearly run, the struggle is all but over; he is weary, as it were, and panting with the effort; but he is success-

[1] 2 Thess. iii. 1. [2] 2 Tim. iv. 7, 8.

ful; the crown is in sight, and the Judge, the "righteous" Judge, who cannot make a mistake, is there, ready to place that bright wreath upon his head.

And as with the word "course," so with the verb that corresponds with it.[1] "It is not of him that willeth, nor of him that *runneth,*" says St. Paul in an argument,[2] which turns all our confidence toward Him who "hath compassion" and "showeth mercy." His anxiety regarding the success of his own apostolic work is expressed by the same image in two very different Epistles, written at widely separated points of time. He tells the Galatians that at an early period he negotiated very carefully at Jerusalem, "lest by any means he *should run* or *had run* in vain;"[3] and writing long afterwards from Rome to the Philippians, he expresses his desire that they may be consistent, in order that he himself "may rejoice in the day of Christ, that he has not *run* in vain."[4] And the metaphor which he applies to the progress of the Gospel committed to him, he applies also to the practical consistency and progress of those who had learnt the truth from him. "Ye did *run* well," he says to some, who had grievously failed and fallen; "who hath hindered you, that ye should not obey the truth?"[5] "Ye were running the Chris-

[1] In 2 Thess. iii. 1, the margin has "run." No use is here made of Heb. xii. 1, simply because in these essays it is not desirable absolutely to assume the Pauline authorship of that Epistle.

[2] Rom. ix. 15, 16.

[3] Gal. ii. 2.

[4] Phil. ii. 16.

[5] Gal. v. 7.

tian race successfully and well; who put these obstacles in your way, which have thrown you down, and brought you to shame?" The whole language, as read in the original Greek, is far more easily recognized as applicable to the foot-race, than can possibly be perceived in the English version.

Thus we see that both direct and indirect advantages may be gained, by pursuing a narrow line of thought suggested by mere words. We here perceive the harmony of St. Paul's language in his speeches and his letters, and lay hold on one of the small collateral proofs of the genuine and honest character both of the Acts and the Epistles. We are very far, however, as yet from having mentioned all instances of the use of such metaphors in these latter documents; and perhaps their use, in fact, strikes us all the more, when the actual words, to which our attention has hitherto been given, are not employed. Thus, when St. Paul says to Timothy, "Exercise thyself unto godliness,"[1] the word he employs is most distinctly taken from the training and practicing for *gymnastic* contests. And then he adds: "Bodily exercise profiteth little, but godliness is profitable unto all things, having the promise of the life that now is, and of that which is to come,"[2] — a passage often misinterpreted. It is, in fact, frequently distorted in two ways. The "bodily exercise" is taken to mean religious asceticism, and the contrast is understood to lie between this and some supposed

[1] 1 Tim. iv. 7. [2] Ver. 8.

"godliness" not connected with bodily self-denial; whereas the comparison is simply between the training of the body for the games, and the training of the whole man, body, soul, and spirit, in the life of religion. And this helps us to avoid the other mistake, which is often committed in the interpretation of the passage. It would be a strange thing, if St. Paul were to urge his disciple to the practice of a strict religious training of his character, by any promise relating chiefly to this life. He does nothing of the kind. He points out that, if the athletes will do so much for a reward which is merely of this world, we ought to do much under the influence of a promise which relates not merely to this world, but also to the next. God has indeed a blessing for this world, as the blessing of Esau; but his highest blessing is for the next world, even as the blessing of Jacob. It is as if St. Paul said to Timothy (and we could well imagine that such recollections of the past were in his mind as he wrote), "My son Timothy, thou rememberest how, when we were at Corinth,[1] with our brother Silas, and Crispus, the ruler of the synagogue, we watched the athletes training for the games; young men of noble forms, eager and active, patient and persevering. It was a foolish toil, for a worthless reward. But we may learn a serviceable lesson from them. The children of this world are in their generation more diligent than the children of light. Train thyself — thy religious character — with

[1] Acts xviii. 5, 8.

the like eagerness and activity, patience and perseverance. Thy reward is not only earthly, but heavenly." And similar trains of thought might be followed in reference to other phrases, where not obviously at first sight, but still really, images from the games are imbedded in the context of the Epistles. Thus, when he says that he himself has spoken the Gospel of God "with much contention,"[1] or that others have been "striving fervently"[2] in intercessory prayer, or when he tells Timothy to "fight the good fight of faith,"[3] the metaphor is really *agonistic*, though the variations in the English version conceal the fact. But we must turn now to more copious passages, where the agonistic allegory is presented in its most animated form.

In the Epistle to the Philippians St. Paul writes thus: "Not as though I had already attained, either were already perfect, — but I follow after. This one thing I do, forgetting those things which are behind, and reaching forth unto those things which are before, I press toward the mark for the prize of the high calling of God in Christ Jesus."[4] Was there ever a more vigorous picture of a runner in earnest? Here is the eager pressing toward a definite end in view, — the feeling that nothing else is to be thought of for the present, the determination that nothing shall interfere with the matter in hand; and at the same time, with this strong effort of the will, there is the

[1] 1 Thess. ii. 2.
[2] Col. iv. 12.
[3] 1 Tim. vi. 12.
[4] Phil. iii. 12–14.

utmost alacrity and activity of movement. Here is no looking back, no thought of giving up the struggle. The whole energy of mind and body is bent upon success; and till success is achieved, nothing is done. It would be easy to dwell on these points at greater length; but really the best commentary on the passage is supplied by the familiar facts of a well contested foot-race.

And there is yet a still more copious and lively instance of the same kind of illustration. As in the discussions of the other metaphors, some one passage was selected as furnishing the best sample, and as containing in fact the main basis for the discussion, so here we turn naturally to some verses in the ninth chapter of the First Epistle to the Corinthians: "Know ye not that they which run in a race, run all, but one receiveth the prize? So run, that ye may obtain. And every man that striveth for the mastery is temperate in all things. Now they do it that they may obtain a fading crown; but we an unfading. I therefore so run, not as uncertainly; so fight I, not as one that beateth the air: but I keep under my body, and bring it into subjection; lest that by any means, when I have preached to others, I myself should be a castaway."[1] It may perhaps be a help toward our entering fully into the spiritual meaning of this passage, if we try to associate one practical topic with each one of the four verses.

And the topic which we may associate with the first

[1] 1 Cor. ix. 24–27.

of the verses is this: the *earnestness of purpose* that is essential to the Christian's career. "Know ye not that they which run in a race, run all, but one receiveth the prize? So run, that ye may obtain." St. Paul appeals to the *experience* of the Corinthians. There was nothing with which they were better acquainted than these famous foot-races. Their own games near their own city were among the most celebrated in the world. They "knew" well that each race was eagerly contested, and that "one" obtained the prize. But at this point we must mark a difference. In that race there was competition; and because there was competition, each runner was in earnest. In the Christian race there is no competition. The prize is within the reach of all. But then each runner must be as much in earnest as though there were competition and only one prize. And this is what the Apostle expresses. He does not say (as I understand his words) "run *so—in such a way—as to* obtain,"—but, "run *so—as those runners run—in order that* ye may obtain." In their case there is rivalry, and therefore they are in earnest. In your case there is no rivalry; but their earnestness of purpose is an example to you.

And certainly no pattern of earnestness can be a more forcible example than the earnestness that arises from eager competition. "Run in the Christian race as the athlete in the foot-race runs." All his nerves and sinews are strung up for the effort he is making. Nothing else is thought of; and as the distance between his feet and the winning-post diminishes, he does not flag, but throws more and more exertion into the movement of his limbs. Whatever strength and elasticity he can summon up, whatever struggling remainder of his short and failing breath he can muster, all may be wanted at the very last moment. And what a contrast this is to our dull and languid Christianity! We go and take our place in the course as though the prize could be won without any running at all, or as if there were no prize worth running for. We dream and loiter and fold our arms; we turn aside to look at every object of passing interest; or if we did begin with some vigor, all the zest and warmth of the struggle grows feebler and fainter when it ought to become more animated, and, like the Galatians, we care little what hindrances occur to stop our course, and to risk a dishonorable fall. Earnestness of purpose is what we want, and there is no picture of earnestness more forcible than that which is drawn from the ardor of competition.

But now we pass to the next verse, "Every man that striveth for the mastery is temperate in all things;" and the lesson is pointed by a contrast, "They do it to obtain a corruptible crown, but we an incorruptible." The successful athlete in the Greek foot-race received for his prize a crown of green leaves, placed by the judge upon his head. In itself it was of no value; but it was the mark of victory. The winning of this crown was sung in poetry; it was the subject of pride and congratulation to the city from which the successful runner came; and it was the ground of boasting for long generations afterwards in his family. For the winning of this, exertions were made involving the utmost patience and self-denial, and no waste of strength and activity was thought too great if only it could be secured. And yet it was only a corruptible, a fading crown. Its beauty passed away sooner than the beauty of those leaves which are stripped off from our trees by the winds of November. And indeed *all* human glory is a fading crown. It *must* wither and die in the end. Yet what trouble men take to obtain it! And what an example in this respect is the eager lover of glory to the Christian! His crown can never fade. To lose that crown, as it certainly may be lost, by neglect, by indolence, by turning out of the right course, by falling headlong over temptations that lie before our very feet, this is surely the strangest and most unaccountable folly; while to win it is worth far more, ten thousand times, than all the toil of the most faithful servant of Christ, all the torture of the most suffering martyr.

This verse, however, points not to suffering, but to self-restraint, which self-restraint is itself a blessing; and the topic which we may associate with these words in the Apostle's comparison might be expressed thus, — *self-restraint inspired by hope.* It is often worth a man's while to give up something which he values for the sake of some higher good in prospect. This is what was done in the Greek athletic

THEATRE AT EPHESUS.

sports when the competitors were under training; and so indeed it is now, sometimes to an absurd extent, in English athletic sports. Classical authors furnish us with materials, by help of which we might, if it were necessary, describe the strict discipline to which these young Greeks were subjected under the trainer,—the diet, the exercise, the hard life, the fixed hours, the peremptory abstinence from everything likely to hinder the end in view. It is the *example* to the *Christian* presented by this discipline which is the point before us. Nor is this the only place where the same Apostle makes a similar reference. In writing another of his Epistles, he says, "If a man also strive for masteries, yet is he not crowned, except he strive lawfully;"[1] *i. e.*, he cannot obtain the prize unless he complies with the regulations; and these regulations included, among other things, very strict and systematic methods of discipline and training. And the gospel strife with earthly sin for a heavenly prize has likewise its strict regulations. There is a preparatory discipline and training to which the Christian must be subjected before he can be fit to enter on his reward. The discipline, however, is, as was said before, itself a blessing. The training is a training for happiness. The Apostle expresses it thus: "Temperance in all things;" the habit of self-restraint running through the whole life; a check placed, not only on the passions, but on the words; moderation strictly practiced in food and in

[1] 2 Tim. ii. 5.

sleep; those eager desires for amusement and novelty kept in control; so that the man is always master of himself. Thus under God's grace that character is formed, which commands respect and exerts influence in this life, and is prepared to enter on the future life, where no sin and folly disturb the balance of the purified soul. It is the hope of that life which furnishes the motive for self-restraint, just as the hope of victory in the foot-race gives the athlete patience to submit to all the discipline and training required by the rules.

"I therefore so run, not as uncertainly; so fight I, not as one that beateth the air," is the next of the Apostle's sentences. *Definiteness of aim*, then, in the Christian's race and contest, is our next topic. And it will be observed, that St. Paul presents this subject under two images: one drawn from running, the other from boxing. The foot-race was as I have said, the most popular athletic contest among the Greeks; and it supplied to the Apostle his favorite comparison, in connection with subjects of this class. But the *pugilistic* contest was also constant and familiar at the public games, and he combines this contest with the other in illustration of the point which is now before us. Not only does the Christian act with earnestness of purpose, not only is he encouraged to practice self-restraint, but he is definite in his aims. And in two ways he is definite. He has a distinct view of the objects of his desire, and a distinct view of the enemies against which he must contend.

"I so run, not as uncertainly." A man who does not know his own mind is seldom successful. That is a very unhappy temperament which is easily turned this way and that, and which always yields to the latest influence, is always persuaded by the last new argument. Such a man is continually in the hands of others. He is never his own master. He never does anything well. And there is another very unhappy habit of mind: when a man does not go direct to his point, — when he tries experiments on the right and on the left; when he loses time by hesitation, or follows circuitous methods, whereas the straightforward course is always the best. They are both opposed to the true dignity of Christian principle. The disciple of Christ should be known as a simple-hearted man. His eye is single. He has one great object before him. His desire is to be like Christ, to prepare for spending eternity with that Blessed Master, and meanwhile to honor Him by doing good to all around him. And nothing could express this in a more lively manner than the comparison with the runner in a race. Direct; with the goal straight before him; with his whole frame vigorously moving that way; moving, too, by the shortest path, — such is his course. Let such be our course. "Forgetting the things that are behind, and reaching forward to the things that are before, let us press toward the mark of the prize of our high calling."

But still, while we have a course to run, we have also enemies to fight; and, to express this, another metaphor is appropriate: "So fight I, not as one that beateth the air." St. Paul passes here from the runner to the boxer, and, drawing a comparison from this source, he points out that the Christian has very definite antagonists. With the pugilist it is no mere striking for striking's sake, no mere pastime, no dealing of blows in the air for the exercise of the muscles. When the Corinthians or Athenians or Ephesians came in crowds to see their favorite athlete engaged in this contest, it was no showy and unmeaning attitudes that they came to witness, but the vigilant and most active employment of hand and eye for the purpose of victory over an opponent equally active and vigilant. And the best application which we can make for ourselves of this apostolic comparison is this: that we must be on the alert against our besetting sins; that we must keep our attention fixed upon them, and deal our blows steadily against them. Now, in order to do this, we must first know what our besetting sins really are. This is a most serious subject. It is not sin in general that we have to contend against, not the sins of our neighbors, not the sins which we have no temptation to commit, but "the sin which doth so easily beset us."[1] What is that sin? Has the reader discovered his besetting sin? If not, this is not the place for dogmatizing on spiritual things; but it may well be doubted whether it is possible for us to be saved at all, unless we have found out our besetting sin.

[1] Heb. xii. 1.

Now let us consider the last of these four emphatic verses: "I keep under my body, and bring it into subjection: lest that by any means, when I have preached unto others, I myself should be a castaway." The image of the pugilist is still continued here; and we have to observe, first, *what* the Apostle does, and, secondly, *why* he does it. He resists his carnal nature, systematically attacks it, and perseveres till he has subdued it; and this he does under the influence of a salutary fear, lest, whilst he has been made a blessing to others, he himself should fail to obtain the reward. The topic then suggested by this part of the passage might be expressed thus: *persevering effort inspired by fear.*

The simple fact of St. Paul using this image at all is a very grave fact. This pugilistic encounter was no mere light and languid amusement. Very often it was a matter of life and death. And certainly there is something very revolting in the thought of such a combat (whether in Ancient Greece or in Modern England) being made an entertainment for a crowd of spectators. But these Corinthians, Ephesians, and Athenians were heathens, and whatever we may feel on this subject does not affect the strong significance of the Apostle's comparison. It is the intense reality of the struggle which constitutes the point of resemblance. Those heavy blows, dealt by one combatant with tremendous force upon the other, are taken to signify the resolute and incessant warfare which the Christian maintains with whatever is sinful in his human nature. These fleshly inclinations are determined to give *him* no rest, and he is determined to give *them* no rest; and he perseveres till the blows of this opponent become weak and faint, and he is master of the field. This is a very serious picture of the Christian life in one of its aspects; and it shows it to be very different from what it is sometimes supposed to be,—a mere habit of passive acquiescence in certain opinions; a mere decorous compliance with certain rules of society; a mere receiving of impressions from without, unaccompanied by any spring of resolute energy from within.

But it is quite as important, and even more important, to observe the *motive* of the Apostle in this energetic and vigilant resistance. His persevering effort is inspired by *fear*: "I keep under my body, and bring it into subjection: lest that by any means, when I have preached unto others, I myself should be a castaway." "*Lest*"—never was a little word more weighty in any sentence; and the writer makes it more emphatic, by the addition of "*by any means.*" Could there be a more solemn admonition of danger? Here is this great Apostle, to whom the establishment of Christianity in the world is due more than to any one else, telling us that he carried on a watchful and vigorous warfare against his fleshly nature, *for fear lest*, in the midst of all these ministrations, he himself should lose his reward. Well, then, may we fear for ourselves; and, most of all, those amongst us who are actively endeavoring to do spiritual good to others. What thought can go with greater power into the very depths of the conscience than this: "God may be using me for the spiritual good of others, and yet my own heart may not be right; my own soul may not be safe, through the mysterious power of sin in my fleshly nature: I may be falling away farther from God, even while I am drawing others nearer to Him?" It is of course obvious that we are here brought into contact with the doctrines of predestination and election, and that a difficulty arises when such a passage as this is compared with passages supporting these doctrines. It is easy to range texts on both sides of such a controversy as that, and not easy to reconcile them, except by making one set of texts give way to another. And this we have no right to do. With other parts of Scripture before us, we might meditate with advantage on the sweet comfort which is derived from the conviction that those who have placed their souls in the care of Christ are safe, and that no one can pluck them out of that Saviour's hands. But that is not our subject now. We must take the Bible as we find it. St. Paul does most distinctly tell us in this place that *with him* the fear of being "a castaway" was a commanding motive. Hope and fear are the two poles of the Christian's life; and certainly fear has a very conspicuous place in Holy Scriptures. "Be not high-minded, but *fear*." "Pass the time of your sojourning here in *fear*." "Let him that thinketh he standeth *take heed* lest he fall."[1]

[1] Rom. xi. 20; 1 Pet. i. 17; 1 Cor. x. 12.

The general subject of St. Paul's habit of taking metaphorical language from the athletic games is by no means yet exhausted. Even in the context which we have been examining at considerable length, there is at least one other agonistic allusion, which might easily escape notice. When St. Paul speaks in this passage of "having preached to others," the true rendering is, "having been *a herald* to others." And the reference is to that officer in the concourse at the games, whose business it was, with his voice, or with a trumpet, to summon the competitors to the exciting struggle. Much more, too, might be said on various points of detail, which have been only lightly touched, such as the training,[1] the rules,[2] the judge,[3] the prize,[4] the attending spectators,[5] and the jubilant joy[6] with which the victor was received at the close of the race. But it is now time to lay the subject aside; and this short series of papers on St. Paul's illustrative language may be briefly concluded by two reflections, — one of which has reference to the Apostle himself, the other to the Bible at large.

It is impossible not to feel, in pursuing such studies as these, that we have not merely St. Paul's instruction and exhortation, but his personal example, before us. We always feel that we should like to know something of the character of a man who produced such wonderful effects in the world as the Apostle

1 1 Cor. ix. 25; 1 Tim. iv. 7, 8. 2 2 Tim. ii. 5. 3 2 Tim. iv. 8.
4 1 Cor. ix. 24; Phil. iii. 14. 5 1 Cor. iv. 9. 6 Acts xx. 24.

Paul. And certainly, we have no lack of materials for forming a judgment on this subject. Among other things, we have his customary language. A man's customary language (at least if he is a man of mark) generally shows something of his character; and perhaps especially the language which he uses in his letters. For in letter-writing we are free from the disturbing influences of conversation, while yet the personal element is strongly present. Four groups of St. Paul's favorite similes have been before our attention, and perhaps each of them might furnish a suggestion in regard to his character. Thus, in his architectural imagery we might be reminded of his steady adherence to first principles, and of his constructive ability (under God's Spirit) in regard both to doctrine and the Church; while his illustrations drawn from agriculture seem to present him before us in his sympathizing care for the spiritual growth of his converts and his reliance on the exercise of God's beneficent power. But perhaps it is more easy to make this use of the metaphors which he draws from Roman Soldiers and Greek Games. We can hardly be mistaken in believing that by combining them together we obtain an approximate picture of the man. In both cases his references to such subjects are copious, natural, and customary. From this we should conclude that there was something of the Soldier and the Athlete in his moral and religious constitution. And so in truth it was. He had much of what we should call tenacity of character, a great power of elastic recovery when he was beaten back by opposition, a strong will, not deterred by difficulties, and at the same time a remarkable alacrity and versatility and readiness of resource. We know this to have been the case, from the facts of his life; but we see it also in the imagery which he is in the habit of borrowing from the Roman Soldiers and the Greek Games.

As to Scripture in general, the remark which suggests itself in conclusion is this, that the careful student can in every part of it enter upon large and precious trains of thought, and can find a germinating power even in what seem to be its secondary portions. In these short essays we have been following very narrow paths through a very limited portion of God's Word; and yet we have found a good deal to interest and instruct us. It is a great proof of the endless variety and richness of the Bible, if we can gain so much by merely pursuing the course of a peculiar word or a characteristic metaphor. God's Word is like God's World, very varied, very rich, very beautiful. You never know when you have exhausted all its secrets. The Bible, like Nature, has something for every class of mind. As in the phenomena around us there are resources and invitations both for science and for poetry, so does God's Revelation furnish materials both for exact theological definition and for the free play of devout thought and feeling. Look at the Bible in a new light, and you straightway see some new charm. This is true, even in regard to very minute particulars. The view from a commanding Alpine summit, which has been climbed by great labor, and where half a kingdom is spread before you, is very glorious and not to be forgotten; but the quiet footpath along the slopes of the lower eminences may also be full of beauty at every turn. And such has been our modest course in these essays. It is something to have obtained a deeper conviction than before of the inexhaustible charms and advantages of even the by-ways of Scripture.

THE COMPANIONS OF ST. PAUL.

PREFACE.

I HAVE long cherished the hope of writing a book on *Scripture Characters.* The biographical form in which a large part of the Bible is given to us is an invitation to this study; and there can be no doubt that, of all studies, it is one of the most instructive.

Yet the books are very few which supply anything like an exhaustive treatment of this subject. Sermons and essays, no doubt, there are in abundance on special characters of Holy Writ; but I know nothing which has any claim to completeness, except Niemeyer's "Charakteristik der Bibel," which first appeared in 1775, and the three volumes of "Scripture Biography," published between 1832 and 1848, by my revered friend Archdeacon Evans. The former work is very unequal; and on other grounds it may be questioned whether a mere translation of it would be the best mode of presenting the whole subject to English readers. The latter work, too, excellent as it is, leaves much to be done in the same field by others.

It seems very unlikely that leisure will ever be granted to me for the accomplishing of what I have desired; but I may hope, if life is prolonged, to publish some slight volumes in illustration of Bible Biography. These papers, which originally appeared in the "Sunday Magazine," and are now republished after revision, are obviously quite superficial, and aim almost exclusively at the promotion of practical religious life. The 1st, 2d, 3d, 7th, and 8th were in substance preached in Chester Cathedral. They will be followed by a new edition of the Hulsean Lectures for 1862, on the "Character of St. Paul," and by some Sermons on Scripture Characters, which have been preached on public occasions.

J. S. H.

CHESTER, *December* 30, 1870.

CONTENTS

THE

COMPANIONS OF ST. PAUL.

I.

ST. BARNABAS.

"A good man, and full of the Holy Ghost and of faith." — ACTS xi. 24.

IN order to study intelligently the character of any man, it is essential to take into account, not only the distinguishing features of his own mind and disposition, but also the circumstances of every kind by which he was surrounded. Those circumstances limit and direct the action of his personality; and they very often make him, in the lapse of time, to be different from what he was at the first. The place where he was born, the scenes that environed his childhood, the occupations in which his faculties have been engaged, all such things have much to do with our estimate of the man himself. And if we suppose that, in later years, he finds a home in a new country, that his health is impaired by climate or other causes, that employments different from the former have begun to occupy his attention, it is evident that the course of his biography must vary accordingly.

Of all the circumstances which surround a man, those which determine his relation to other men are by far the most important. The companions even of the greatest man may almost be said to be constituent parts of his character. They must certainly be known and appreciated, before we can give a truthful and complete account of his career. A man's companions receive his influence and reflect his feelings; through them he necessarily acts on society at large; and, again, they react powerfully upon his own sentiments, and frequently modify the form of his work. We cannot isolate him from them without the risk of distorting, and either dwarfing or exaggerating, his proportions.

These remarks are preëminently true of such a person as the Apostle Paul, whose temperament was preëminently social. This feature of his mind and heart is conspicuous everywhere, whether we study him in his own Epistles, or in the narrative written by his friend St. Luke. The human environment, so to speak, which surrounds St. Paul, is the very atmosphere of his life. We cannot separate him from his companions. By seeing his power over them we see what he was. In his relations to them, on the one hand, we trace the delicate shades of his fine feeling. On the other hand, they were the instruments by which he acted on large communities. It is true likewise, that, charged though he was with a Divine commission and empowered inwardly with supernatural strength, yet his companions had a reflex action upon his feelings and habits of thought. In contact with them his human characteristics were developed, as literally as might be the case with any of ourselves; and they frequently determined the course of his conduct and shaped the results of his life.

A series of papers, then, on the "Companions of St. Paul," may be of some little value as contributing toward the illustration of the Great Apostle's own biography, independently of the utility of studying these men and women themselves. Such a series, in an unpretending form, I now propose to offer to the reader; and in doing this my aim will be, not simply to bring out to view the characteristics of St. Paul's associates, one by one, but also to make some useful applications of them, so as to put various parts of our own experience, in succession, side by side with their examples.

There are two very obvious reasons why we should begin with Barnabas.

In the first place this course is chronologically correct. The intimate associations of St. Paul with this friend began at the very outset of his active career. No earlier companionship is recorded in connection with the Apostle's influence over the minds of others, or the progress of his Missionary work. Moreover, it is more than probable that they were well acquainted with one another before either of them was a Christian. One came from Cyprus; the other from Cilicia;[1] and these two provinces were

[1] Acts iv. 36; xxi. 39; xxii. 3.

closely connected with one another by mercantile intercourse. Paul, too, and Barnabas were both of pure Israelitish descent.[1] Thus not only the geographical circumstances of the case, but the affinities of feeling which would naturally subsist between men, who, while Jews of the Greek dispersion, were yet loyal to the old hereditary Judaism, point to the probability of an early friendship; and certainly the supposition of such a friendship explains much of what is recorded in the Bible concerning the relations of the two men.

But, further, the selection of Barnabas for our first subject is made natural in another way. His kindly disposition, and the service which he rendered to St. Paul, constitute him, above all others in this group, a good representative of personal friendship. If in any one, among the associates of our Apostle, the idea of companionship is, as it were, personified, that one is Barnabas. Something of this characteristic is made known to us in the designation which the earlier Apostles gave to him, when they styled him the "Son of Consolation."[2] It is probable, indeed, that this title had reference chiefly to his power of warm and instructive "exhortation;" but, even if thus interpreted, it reveals to us social qualities of high value; and certainly his actions are in harmony with this power of giving encouragement by his words. And this, too, must be added, as we shall presently see, that Barnabas displays the defective and weak side,

[1] Acts iv. 36; Phil. iii. 5.

[2] Acts iv. 36.

as well as the cheering and consoling side, of an ardent and affectionate disposition.

There are four passages in the New Testament, all connected with St. Paul, which bring before us definite features of the character of Barnabas, — two exhibiting his high excellences, and two revealing his faults. But before we turn to them, we must glance at an earlier passage, which has no reference to the Apostle of the Gentiles, but is valuable to us here as striking the key-note, so to speak, of the character of his friend.

In those happy earliest days of the Church, when "the multitude of them that believed were of one heart and one soul," when none of them said "that aught of the things which he possessed was his own," and consequently "none among them lacked," — Barnabas, "a Levite, of the island of Cyprus," is the one among the disciples who is specified as "selling his land, and laying the price at the Apostles' feet," for the general good of the Christian community.[1] Either the amount which he gave was peculiarly large, or there was something in his manner of giving, which causes him to be singled out in this description of self-denying generosity; and we may pause here for a moment, to note the example which would be afforded to us, even if we were to proceed no further.

Generosity, — we shall find that this word, better than any other, describes the character of Barnabas.

[1] Acts iv. 37.

This first incident from his life exhibits to us generosity in its literal sense of the free surrendering of private property for the public benefit. But this is by no means the main point on which we should lay hold, in striving to learn something from the example. Mere giving may arise from various motives. But the deep inward principle of generosity applies to all the conduct of life, and finds its exercise even when we have no property to give. A generous man is a man whose heart goes out freely and warmly toward others, — who is not always thinking of himself; not calculating nicely how this or that will affect his own comfort, his own credit, his own position. Such a man is always ready for kind and neighborly acts. And such a man, too, can easily throw himself into mutual understanding and combination with others for the general good; whereas a man who is centered in himself is always liable to be mistaken and to mistake those around him. Let me illustrate this by a homely comparison.

There is a characteristic difference between houses in the East and houses in the West. Our dwellings have their windows on the outside, from which we can look on the open country and see freely what is passing elsewhere. A domestic dwelling in the East, on the contrary, opens into an inner court, which presents the only view, while all around is the dull dead wall. There is something of the same kind of difference between one man and another. Some can easily begin frank and open communication with their neighbors — other men cannot or will not. Barnabas is an example of the former; and he was all the happier in consequence, and all the more useful.

And there is another mark of generosity, suggested by the passage before us, which should not be overlooked. A generous man, acting on warm impulses, does not delay in doing good, but acts promptly and on the moment. The help wanted by the Christian community in Jerusalem was wanted then, and Barnabas gave it then. He might very naturally have considered the various reasons there were for delay. For instance, it was probable that similar need for assistance might occur on some future occasion. Besides this, many other persons were giving liberally at that time. But Barnabas did not reason in this way. Probably he did not reason at all. And this at least we may learn from him, that, when undoubted good is to be done, it is best to do it heartily, and to do it now.

But it is time that we should turn to the first of the four passages, which describes circumstances in the life of Barnabas directly connected with St. Paul. Generosity is here again manifest, but in another and a more winning aspect.

It was a most critical moment in St. Paul's life, and in the history of the Church. On his return to Jerusalem, after his sudden conversion at Damascus, he was naturally suspected. "He assayed to join himself to the disciples; but they were all afraid of him, and believed not that he was a disciple."[1] It is difficult to blame them. For what could they have thought of him? Here was a man who had been their unscrupulous enemy, "breathing out slaughter and threatenings," dragging "both men and women into prison,"[2] ready to undergo any toil and travel to any distance, if only he might extirpate the Christians; and now this man was in Jerusalem again, professing to be their friend and wishing to be associated with them. They must have thought it was some contrivance, some stratagem arranged for their harm. It must be remembered that they were not then a powerful body, but very weak, with no protection from the authorities. They were like a flock of sheep; and they might well say of this son of Benjamin, in the words applied to his great ancestor: "He ravins like a wolf; in the morning he devoured the prey; and now at night he is dividing the spoil."[3]

If we consider the crisis, we see how much harm would have come both to St. Paul's personal comfort and happiness, and to his power of extending and consolidating the Church, if this most natural and most serious misunderstanding had not been removed. The happy instrument of removing it was Barnabas. "He took him, and brought him to the Apostles, and declared unto them how he had seen the Lord in the way, and that He had spoken to him, and how he had preached boldly at Damascus in the name of Jesus." The result was entire confidence

[1] Acts ix. 26. [2] Acts ix. 1, 2; xxii. 4. [3] Gen. xlix. 27.

and work heartily combined in the cause of Christ. He who had been a persecutor was now with the Apostles at Jerusalem, as a trusted friend and fellow-laborer, "coming in and going out" and "speaking boldly."

Now I spoke above of putting our experience side by side with the example of Barnabas. Misunderstandings are very common in this poor world of ours. People will differ without reason; will take unfavorable views of one another; will think they are on opposite sides, when really they are not on opposite sides. When such a state of things is seen to arise, this is the great opportunity for those (and they are very numerous) who occupy themselves in gossip and making mischief. But this is also the Christian's opportunity for making peace and promoting combination in good and useful works. Let the reader ask himself what he is in the habit of doing in such a case. A very common habit with us is simply to look on, under such circumstances, and to be passive, — possibly even to take a sort of pleasure in the infirmities of our neighbors. "These people," we say, "*will* look upon one another as enemies, when they ought to be friends; they are very foolish; but we cannot help it"; and we do nothing. Such was not the view or the practice of Barnabas. And this system of letting things grow crooked, when we might do something toward putting them straight, is really moral cowardice or moral laziness; and we must remember that we are responsible, not only for the harm which we positively cause, but also, in a great measure, for the evil which we might have prevented.

Only it must be recollected that whatever good we do in this way must be done, not by harshness and rebuke, but by sympathy and persuasion. This is a principle of almost universal application, and to nothing is it more applicable than to cases of religious misunderstanding. But, most strangely, we are in the habit of forgetting this. We live in a time of much religious debate. And this, indeed, is by no means an unmixed evil. Anything is better than stagnant indifference; and debate has a tendency to bring out truth more clearly into view. If others hold wrong opinions, our wish must be to induce them to adopt right opinions. But is it wise to attempt to secure this end by the method of attack? Let us ask any man to refer to his own experience. Were you ever convinced yourself by being attacked? When you were assailed, was not your first impulse to resist, and to shelter yourself as closely as possible within your old defenses? You have heard the fable of the Traveller, the Wind, and the Sun. The Traveller was enveloped in a thick cloak. The Wind and the Sun contended which of them could most easily induce him to lay the cloak aside. The Wind made the attempt first. A furious storm came over the heavens, the trees were broken, the cattle were terrified, the cold sleet drove angrily across the plain. But the Traveller drew his cloak more closely to him, and folded it round and round. And now the weather cleared. The landscape grew bright again. The Sun's turn was now come to make the attempt. As the warmth of the rays increased, the Traveller gradually relaxed his hold. Each step made him feel that the cloak was more and more a burden; he laid it aside; and the Sun had succeeded, where the Wind had failed. What could never have been done by violent attack, was easily accomplished by gentle persuasion. Barnabas, at a critical time, not by harsh discussion, but by genial warmth, removed a prejudice; and we, following in his steps, may perhaps find many opportunities of doing the same.

Nor is it merely the satisfaction and happiness of religious fellow-workmen which is to be considered in such a case. Simple offices of Christian kindness may be of far greater moment to the community at large than can be calculated at the time. This incident in the life of Barnabas is of peculiar value, because it shows us what great results may follow to the progress of the Gospel from a single act of timely generosity.

The second passage, which sets Barnabas before us in close companionship with the Apostle, leads us to give him a very great place in the Apostolic history, both for a far-seeing and enlightened intelligence, and for a noble and generous nature. News came from Jerusalem that the reception of the Gospel was proceeding with unexampled success in the northern parts of Syria, especially at Antioch.[1] The authorities of the Church felt instinctively that Barnabas was the fittest man to send on a mission of inquiry and encouragement. The account of his feeling and conduct on his arrival at Antioch is replete with information concerning his mind and character. "When he came and had seen the grace of God, he was glad." We recognize here immediately one of those sure indications which are prominent in St. Paul's description of true Christian charity,[2] namely, that it "rejoiceth in the truth." And then follow words which exhibit Barnabas as a "Son of Exhortation." "He exhorted them all, that with purpose of heart they would cleave unto the Lord." In all this there are the clear tokens of a genial, friendly, and zealous disposition. Then, immediately below, it is added, "For he was a good man, and full of the Holy Ghost and of Faith," — a sentence which is placed at the head of this paper, because it seems to concentrate in itself the full description of the man. Those who unite thus the inward power of Divine grace with natural aptitude for persuasion, are commonly successful. And the success of Barnabas at Antioch was great. "Much people was added unto the Lord."

Such occurrences, taking place in a city so populous, and so eminent both in political and mercantile life, were of peculiar moment to the future history of the Church. Barnabas evidently felt the critical value of the opportunity; for he decided to stay at

[1] Acts xi. 22. [2] 1 Cor. xiii. 6.

Antioch. But something of still greater importance follows. He knew of St. Paul's special mission to the Gentiles. He felt how desirable it was that his friend should be brought to labor in the midst of this movement of active thought and serious conviction at Antioch. Accordingly, he "went to Tarsus to seek Saul: and when he had found him he brought him unto Antioch. And it came to pass that a whole year they assembled themselves with the Church, and taught much people."

We cannot dwell too carefully on this transaction, whether we wish to estimate the impulse thus given to the progress of Christianity, or to appreciate the distinctive features of the character of Barnabas. It was at Antioch, under the joint ministry of these two men, that the Church of Christ first became conscious of itself, so to speak, as a great self-existent community, and received its proper designation.[1] From Antioch, too, proceeded the first great missionary expedition of the Church in the persons of these two men.[2] It is, however, rather the individual part played by Barnabas at this time, on which we are here to dwell. His friend, since their last meeting, though fully recognized as a true disciple by the Christians at Jerusalem[3] (and this recognition was due to Barnabas), had been driven away by persecution, and had been living and working in the shade at Tarsus. Certainly we cannot suppose him to have been idle. But it was Barnabas who gave him the

[1] Acts xi. 26. [2] Acts xiii. 4. [3] Gal. i. 22–24.

great opportunity, which was now open before him. Barnabas may be said, in a certain sense, to have made Paul what he afterwards became. He brought him out of obscurity. He put him in the fore-front, though he must have been well aware that he was likely to become more distinguished and powerful than himself. This is that peculiar mark of a generous disposition which was mentioned above, the absence of anxiety for personal credit, the readiness for friendly combination in useful undertakings without any selfish end in view. There are some men who have no heart for any enterprise, unless they can have the first place in it. This is perhaps a prevalent temptation with most energetic characters. But this habit of mind is not according to the law laid down by Christ. "Whosoever will be chief among you, let him be your servant."[1] And Barnabas is a good example to show us how such temptation can be overcome.

We do not wonder at the confidence which he inspired on various occasions, and in reference to very different subjects. Thus, when charitable contributions were soon afterwards sent from Antioch to the poor Christians in Judæa, he was chosen with St. Paul, to convey the gift.[2] At another time, when the two men were engaged in missionary work, and garlands and sacrifices were brought out with the intention of doing worship to the Apostles, the title which these poor idolaters of Lystra gave to Barnabas

[1] Matt. xx. 27. [2] Acts xi. 30.

seems like a recognition of his benignity.[1] And afterwards, when a very serious religious question required to be settled, affecting the whole future condition of Gentile converts, he again was chosen, with three others, to convey the decisive letter from Jerusalem to Antioch; and it is said, in the very phrase which is the translation of his name, that, when the letter was read, "they rejoiced for the Consolation."[2]

But such a character has its defects and its dangers. And now, more briefly, we must take notice of two instances where Barnabas failed in his duty, under the pressure, apparently, of temptations incident to his natural disposition. It would not be fair to the Scriptures, or to Barnabas, or to ourselves, to pass over his failings in silence; not fair to the Scriptures, for they never present to us any biography, except ONE, as absolutely perfect; not fair to Barnabas, for the saints of God are deeply conscious of infirmity and sin, and would not wish to wear a false gloss upon their character; not fair to ourselves, for one of our great encouragements is to know that the Scripture Saints, in whom grace was victorious, were naturally men "of like passions" with us.[3]

The first missionary journey had been happily accomplished; but soon after the close of it a sharp quarrel took place between the two men who had labored so well together. Their companion on the journey, John Mark, a near relative of Barnabas, had been unfaithful in Pamphylia, had shrunk from

[1] Acts xiv. 12. [2] Acts xv. 31. [3] Acts xiv. 15.

the difficulties and dangers of the enterprise, and had returned to his home.[1] We are told, near the end of the fifteenth chapter, that Paul and Barnabas again proposed to "go and visit their brethren in every city where they had preached the word of the Lord, to see how they fared." The strong desire, and, indeed, determination of Barnabas, was to take his young relative along with them once more. "But Paul thought not good to take him with them, who departed from them in Pamphylia, and went not with them to the work; and the contention was so sharp between them, that they departed asunder one from the other," and took different routes.[2]

Thus the friendship which had not been disturbed by selfishness on either side, or by difference of disposition, now gave way before the sensitiveness caused by family relationships. The expression seems to imply that temper was lost on both sides. Therefore, both were to blame. St. Paul's part in the transaction we need not now pause to examine. But we may take occasion to remark that warm-hearted and generous men, like Barnabas, should beware of too much partiality toward relatives, in any case where posts of responsibility are in question. Even religious men are apt to take a very false view of this matter; and ever since the quarrel of these two good men at Antioch, this kind of domestic management has, again and again, both in public appointments and in private matters, brought great discredit on relig-

[1] Acts xiii. 13. [2] Acts xv. 36–40.

ious profession. Many are the occasions when such an appeal as the following might most properly be made: "You may think your relative a very good man for such a post. But your thinking so does not make the fact really so. On the contrary, your judgment in this case is very likely to be under the influence of your feelings. And, after all, the question is, not who is a good man, but who is the best man." It will be observed here, that nothing has been said against promoting the progress in life of the younger members of our families, watching over their interests, and using every effort to start them well, and to encourage them in the path of duty. We know on the highest authority, that "if any provide not for his own house," he is worse than one who has never heard of Christianity.[1] Attention is merely drawn to a distinction which is constantly forgotten in all ranks of life. A post of public trust is not created for the benefit of the man who holds it, but the benefit of those whom he is to serve in that post. Therefore our conduct in such cases should be guided, not by our affections and our preferences, but by our desire for the public good. There is little doubt that St. Paul was right on the whole; though certainly he ought to have kept his temper. And perhaps his firmness on this occasion had a most beneficial effect on the young man himself, who is declared, many years afterwards, to have then become "profitable for the ministry." [2]

[1] 1 Tim. v. 8.

[2] 2 Tim. iv. 11.

But another instance of weakness on the part of Barnabas is recorded in Holy Scripture. The last passage to which reference has been made is found in one of the Epistles. He and St. Paul had at least one other meeting in the same famous city of Antioch. There is every reason to believe that the old quarrel had entirely passed away, and that the unflinching Apostle of the Gentiles and the generous-hearted kinsman of Mark [1] were firm friends again. But once more, and at the same place, a painful occurrence brought the two friends into open collision. We need not inquire here into the precise date of the event, or describe the circumstances out of which it arose. We are merely considering Barnabas in his relation to St. Paul. It is in the Epistle to the Galatians that the transaction is recorded.[2] St. Paul is alluding to an occasion when St. Peter was very much to blame, and seriously in danger of promoting wide-spread corruption of the truth. This too was a critical time. It was of peculiar importance just then to maintain the principles of the Gospel clearly, and without any chance of mistake; and St. Peter had wrongly given apparent sanction to those who were mixing Jewish error with the truth. This had a disastrous effect on those who were within reach of his influence. "The other Jews dissembled likewise with him; insomuch that Barnabas also was carried away with their dissimulation."

It is apparently not difficult to trace here the char-

[1] Col. iv. 10. [2] Gal. ii. 11.

acteristic temperament of Barnabas again on its weak side. His was just that kind of disposition which makes it easy to become a partisan, to flow on with the general current, to take the complexion of surrounding opinion, and to sanction by acquiescence many things which ought to be resisted. It is not pleasant for a warm-hearted and generous man to tell his neighbors that they are all in the wrong. When there is ready facility for giving and winning confidence and for securing coöperation, there must also be the danger of easy yielding, in order to please. But we may carry this trustful and uninquiring acquiescence so far, that it becomes unfaithfulness; and then harm results instead of good. The desire to make everything smooth with everybody is a temptation to be most resolutely resisted. It is quite true that St. Paul tells us that he himself "pleased all men in all things;"[1] but this was in opposition to pleasing himself; and he adds that he pleased them for their "profit, that they might be saved." The pleasing was not the end, but the means. It is true also that he "was made all things to all men;"[2] but the conclusion of the sentence must be examined too, that we may see the correct meaning of these words. It was in order that "by all means he might save some." If our end is the saving of men's souls, we shall find that resistance is sometimes a duty as well as acquiescence. And certainly the tolerating of erroneous human admixtures

[1] 1 Cor. x. 33. [2] 1 Cor. ix. 22.

with Revealed Truth is not the way to save men's souls. St. Paul felt this very deeply, and therefore he gave a severe rebuke to St. Peter, and indirectly gave a salutary admonition to Barnabas, and to all who, like Barnabas, are tempted, even by generous and unselfish feelings, to join with those who are unfaithful to the cause of Christ.

Now we have been looking at the faults of Barnabas. We have not disguised those faults, but have honestly followed the record of the New Testament in exposing them to view. But let not this be the last impression left on our minds. Let our thoughts go back, at the close of these remarks, and rest upon his good qualities; his generosity in giving whatever he could give to increase the happiness and comfort of those around him, and in giving it heartily and without delay; his generosity in taking trouble to remove misunderstandings, to promote coöperation, and to establish friendship among those who were in danger of becoming enemies; his generosity in rejoicing over the spiritual attainments of others, in the absence of envy and jealousy, and in willingness to take the lowest place, if only he might be useful. Let this example be taken into our hearts, so that we may strive, by God's grace, to imitate it, and thus become, among those who surround us, "Sons of Consolation, with messages of love; Daughters of Consolation, on loving errands, too." [1]

[1] See Hymn for St. Barnabas' Day, in the *Church's Year*, by the Bishop of Lincoln.

"Sons of Consolation," "Daughters of Consolation." It is a Hebrew form of expression, and denotes that the wish to give consolation is close to the heart, and that efforts to give consolation are the habit of the life. None of us, however, can be the real fountain-head of consolation. "Christ the Consoler" is seated *alone* in the midst of suffering Humanity.[1] In order to bring true consolation, we must point to Him. Before his gracious countenance the chains of the captive fall off. In his tender sympathy, the heart that has been wounded by sorrow finds relief. In his strengthening presence the distracted mind recovers its balance. Through Him sin is forgiven. May God enable us all to "flee for refuge to lay hold upon the hope set before us;" for here only — whatever alleviations there may be for a time, here only, for time and for eternity — is "Strong Consolation."[2]

1 The allusion is to Ary Scheffer's well-known picture, "Christus Consolator."

2 Heb. vi. 18.

II.

LYDIA.

"Whose heart the Lord opened, that she attended unto the things which were spoken of Paul." — ACTS xvi. 14.

THERE is always a peculiar interest in examining the first beginnings of an enterprise which has resulted in great success. While contemplating the results with satisfaction, and looking over the wide range of all that has been accomplished, we find our thoughts inevitably suggesting the question, What were the characteristics of the first steps in that which has made such remarkable progress?

There is no doubt that one of the greatest and most successful enterprises of the world has been the extending of Christianity over Europe. For centuries, with one small exception, every country in this Continent has been, at least nominally, Christian. And with its Christianity have grown up that civilization and that power of Europe which are too often made the occasions of foolish boasting. But all this state of things had once a beginning. When St. Paul was in that part of his history which corresponds with this sixteenth chapter of the Acts, *i. e.*, about twenty years after the death and resurrection of Christ, there was no Christianity at all in Europe, except so far as a few scattered Jews, travelling for purposes of trade, — or here and there a Greek sailor or Roman soldier, — might have in their hearts the seeds of Divine truth, sown there by the words and work of Christ in Judæa, or elsewhere by some followers of Christ. No doubt in this way some preparation was going on for the great Christian community of Rome; but still, on the whole, it may be said with truth that Europe at this moment was Heathen from one end to the other.

The circumstances, therefore, of the first passing of our religion from Asia into Europe, invest this portion of Sacred History with surpassing interest. In reading it, we find ourselves in the midst of the first days of an enterprise which grew continually from that point, and which has resulted in an astonishing success. And this we may say at once of the characteristics of these earliest days of European Christianity, that they come before us in Scripture with an impression of peculiar cheerfulness. This can be made evident in more ways than one. It strikes us forcibly, in the first place, if we compare the circumstances of this time with those of the time immediately preceding.

St. Paul had been travelling through Galatia. We see this from the sixth verse. There it seems that he was struck down and delayed by an attack of illness. He mentions this afterwards in writing to the Galatians, "Ye know how through infirmity of the flesh I preached the Gospel to you at the first;" or, more correctly and more fully, "Ye remember that I was in weak health when I was among you preaching the Gospel at the first, and, in fact, that weak health was the cause of my stay among you;" and then he proceeds to remind them of their sympathy with his sufferings.[1] The tone in which he writes this shows that he felt the trial very deeply. Now, in coming down from Galatia to the coast of Troas, he met St. Luke. This we know beyond any doubt, from the form of the narrative. Again, in another of his Epistles we find him describing St. Luke as "the beloved physician." [2] And it always seems to me that we ought to connect together this sickness and this meeting with the physician. However this may be, the Apostle did meet at Troas, at this particular time, a congenial spirit and an honest friend, who thenceforward shared his toil and cheered him with his society. But to this subject we shall return in the next of this series of papers on "The Companions of St. Paul."

And in another way, if we read the narrative correctly, we see how cheerful circumstances attended this crossing over into Europe, as compared with what had occurred immediately before. On leaving Galatia there had been much perplexity and disappointment. They attempted to preach the Gospel in one district, and were prevented. They "assayed" to go into another district, "but the Spirit suffered them not."[3] In what particular form these hin-

[1] Gal. iv. 13. [2] Col. iv. 14. [3] Acts xvi. 6, 7.

drances presented themselves we are not informed, but the effect must have been great discouragement; and to a man of St. Paul's temperament, especially after recent illness, it must have been peculiarly trying to make no progress. But on reaching the seacoast at Troas, an express vision made everything clear. There appeared to the Apostle, in the night, a man of Macedonia, saying, "Come over"—into Europe—"and help us." So the clouds, which had hung over their path, now rolled away. The course, which had been obscure, now became distinctly visible. "Immediately," said St. Luke, "we endeavored to go into Macedonia, assuredly gathering that the Lord had called us to preach the Gospel there."[1] *We* endeavored, it must be observed, is the expression used. The "*we*" is not employed in describing what happened in Galatia, or on the way from thence to Troas. This is the proof, which was referred to above, that St. Luke became St. Paul's companion at this particular point.

Even the short description of the voyage leaves a most cheerful impression upon the mind. "Loosing from Troas, we came with a straight course to Samothracia, and the next day to Neapolis, and from thence to Philippi." There was no delay. If they sailed with a straight course, the wind must have been favorable. And as to the time spent on the passage, we have a subsequent account of the same voyage occupying five days, whereas on this occasion it took only

[1] Acts xvi. 10.

parts of two.[1] Those who remember how various the intervals of time used to be in the early part of this century, according to the weather, in the crossing over between Holyhead and Dublin, can judge how well worth while it is to allude to all such circumstances.

But now we are brought to Philippi, where a flourishing and admirable Church was speedily founded. This was the beginning of Christianity in Europe. We were to examine more particularly the characteristics of the first steps in an enterprise so great and successful.

The facts are given very simply thus (vers. 13–15): "We were in that city" — Philippi — "abiding certain days. And on the Sabbath we went out of the city by a river side, where prayer was wont to be made; and we sat down, and spake unto the women which resorted thither. And a certain woman named Lydia, a seller of purple, of the city of Thyatira, which worshipped God, heard us: whose heart the Lord opened, that she attended unto the things which were spoken of Paul. And when she was baptized, and her household, she besought us saying, If ye have judged me to be faithful to the Lord, come into my house, and abide there. And she constrained us."

(1.) First, then, I notice that the whole of this great success began with *prayer*. Just as at the beginning of what we may call Asiatic Christianity in Jerusalem, immediately, after our Lord's ascension, the

[1] Compare Acts xvi. 11 with xx. 6.

Apostles, "with the women, continued with one accord in prayer and supplication," so here, at the beginning of European Christianity, prayer is the preliminary step, before any true progress is made. And it is not merely the *act* of prayer that attracts our attention at this point, but the *habit* of prayer. Lydia and her friends gathered together in the place "where prayer was wont to be made." Provision was carefully made for a serious employment; a place was fixed for the purpose; an engagement was kept. It is a most instructive example; and the more closely we look at it, the more we see how applicable it is to ourselves in regard to all our undertakings. In every missionary enterprise, in every effort to improve and extend religious work around us, in the education of the young, in our common daily employments, in our time of adversity, in our time of prosperity, — if we are to hope for God's blessing we must begin with prayer.

(2.) A further point should now be remarked, namely, the day on which these meetings for prayer took place. I have observed that arrangements were made for a fixed day, and the rule punctually kept. And the day from which all this missionary success spread forth was the *Sabbath*. From this I draw an inference as to the blessing which comes from a religious observance of our English Sunday. It is true that, in this narrative, we have merely to do with the Jewish Sabbath. It was on Saturday, as we should say, that Lydia and the other women met by the river side for prayer at Philippi, just as other Jews met in their synagogues on Saturday at Thessalonica or at Corinth. The Easter sun had not yet risen upon Europe. But the principle which actuated them is the same principle which should influence our conduct. It was the keeping of an appointed day holy. It was the conscientious use of a well-known opportunity for religious benefit.

Now, it is possible that among the readers of these essays there may be some — and let me single out especially young men — who, either at the present time or at some future time, may be under circumstances which tempt them to disregard God's Holy Day. There may be ridicule to be feared, or there may be the enticements of pleasure or of business. The example of these godly women is good for such cases. They had moral courage to do what they felt to be right and good for their souls. The day appointed for religious rest was not neglected. And the example, too, is full of encouragement as well as warning. For the great Christian harvest which began in the flourishing Church of Philippi, grew from the seeds sown on these Sabbath days.

(3.) But the text now calls us to lay stress on another point; and here the example becomes more personal and individual. At these meetings there was "a certain woman named Lydia, whose heart the Lord opened, so that she attended unto the things which were spoken of Paul." Here is the operation of *grace*, — of the Divine grace which comes in answer to prayer and in the use of appointed means. The inward power of religion can be derived only from this source. By preaching an earnest sermon we can produce an impression on the ear; by writing a religious book we can produce an impression on the eye; but the effectual reception of the truth in the mind, the warm action of the truth upon the heart, this is due to God alone. "The Lord opened the heart of Lydia, that she attended unto the things which were spoken of Paul." We cannot lay too much stress upon the manner in which Lydia's change is described to us. It is from this living spring alone that the fertilizing stream of true Christianity flows. When we read in the Scriptures the history of the outward growth of the Church, this is the underthought which is always present. When we ourselves are discussing the means and methods of doing good, we must never forget that all true progress is urged on, through us, by the Divine hand. It is well, and, indeed, quite necessary, that we should spend diligent efforts in the increase and strengthening of religious ministrations all around us. But let such efforts always be associated with prayer, that Divine grace, as in the instance of Lydia, may accompany such ministrations, and make them powerful in saving souls.

(4.) And now let us observe further how *quiet* this beginning was. This is a fourth and a very instructive characteristic. "The kingdom of God cometh not with observation."[1] Here, in the first

[1] Luke xvii. 20.

steps of the Christian religion on the Continent of Europe, is no great conspicuous movement, no ostentatious parade. Here is not even a great assembly gathered together, so that a public appeal might be made, and an impression produced on a whole community. That little assembly by the river side was as simple and unobtrusive as possible, more like a small prayer-meeting, or a Bible class, or a cottage lecture, as we might say, than anything else. There had been great and conspicuous movements on those shores. Conquering armies had passed this way, and history records proudly all the particulars. The contrast is great with what we read here. St. Luke's simple record tells us of something altogether modest and unpretending. These few women, meeting thus for prayer at the river side, were probably almost less regarded than any other inhabitants of Philippi. On these Sabbath days, the occupations of the city went on as usual, — Roman soldiers on parade, women coming in from the country to market, shopkeepers at their business, the magistrates administering justice; and then, as the evening came on, general, and not very innocent amusement. Meantime these godly women sought out a quite place, retired from all the distractions of the town, and prayed; and in this unpretending scene the Conversion of Europe began.

There is much encouragement in this. Only few of us can fill any great place in the world; and if more of us could fill such a place, possibly the religious results might be very small. But here is something very modest in its beginning, very large in its results. This reminds us that, not parade and display, but godly simplicity, is the sure guarantee of success. All of us, however humble in position, can reproduce in our own life an experience like that of Lydia and her companions at Philippi; and in so doing we may be the precursors of blessing on a far greater scale than we imagine. The brightest light may begin in a spark. The largest tree grows from a seed. In "quietness and confidence" is "strength."[1]

(5.) But observe further — and this, too, is a very practical point for our modern English life — that all who assembled thus for prayer and became the first European disciples of St. Paul, were *women*. At least, no men are mentioned. "We went out," says St. Luke, "where prayer was wont to be made: and we sat down, and spake to the women which resorted thither." And the one who is specified as having her "heart opened" by the Lord, in consequence of what was spoken, is a woman.

It would seem also that the Christian work of women was characteristic of this Church at Philippi. In the Epistle addressed to it long afterwards, we find St. Paul saying, "Help those women who labored with me in the Gospel;" and an observable message is sent in that letter to two of the Christian women in this place. "I beseech Euodia and beseech Syntyche, that they be of the same mind in the Lord."[2] How similar this hint is to what is very often required

[1] Is. xxx. 15. [2] Phil. iv. 2.

among ourselves! Here are two good women, engaged, no doubt, in works of religious usefulness; but they cannot agree. Some family misunderstanding — some silly party spirit — some infirmity of temper — has spoilt their coöperation and diminished the usefulness of their lives. Thus does the Bible mingle for us here, as elsewhere, admonition with its encouragement.

I think we may go further, and say that this help of women seems to have been characteristic of the Churches founded in Europe. At Antioch in Pisidia, indeed, the leading women of the city are conspicuous, but as hinderers and persecutors, not as promoters of St. Paul's work.[1] But in every one of the great European Churches women are in the forefront as helpers of the Gospel. From Philippi the Apostle went to Thessalonica. There we find "the chief women not a few" among the true and active believers.[2] From thence to Athens. There of two converts who are specified by name, one was a woman.[3] From Athens to Corinth; and there, and in its neighborhood, we encounter the familiar names of Chloe, Priscilla, and Phœbe, two of whom, at least, must come more particularly before our notice hereafter;[4] while in the great Epistle to Rome, written from Corinth, the enumeration of female converts — mentioned, too, in terms which show that they were active laborers in the good cause — is very remarkable.[5]

1 Acts xiii. 50. 2 Acts xvii. 4. 3 Acts xvii. 34.
4 Rom. xvi. 1; 1 Cor. i. 11; xvi. 19. 5 Rom. xvi. 3–15.

Why do I lay stress on this fact? It is that I may make the example of Lydia all the stronger, by showing that it is not an isolated one, —that I may use the whole case as an argument addressed to women, and that I may say to them, "See what you can do for the Gospel, if you try. Do you wish to promote its acceptance and its influence? If you do, you can. Probably you can really do even more than men." In the state of society of which we read in the Acts of the Apostles, women were, in the very nature of the case, the best Missionaries. And the same thing will be felt now to be true in regard to the Mohammedan world, if we are to convert it at all. But at home also the same thing is true. The phrase "Home Missions" expresses very well what we are continually wanting, even in our families. The Church is, in a great measure, only nominally converted: it needs missionary effort thrown continually in upon itself; and the best workers in its field must still be such as these godly women of the New Testament.

(6.) We are thus brought to another point, which is also conspicuous as one of the characteristic features of this early European Church, namely, that it was preëminently the religion of *household life.* It is, in fact, here first that the conversion of households is mentioned in the Acts of the Apostles. But it is mentioned here very emphatically The narrative proceeds to inform us, immediately after the text, that Lydia "was baptized, and her household." The blessing which came to her diffused itself over the whole circle of her domestic life. And the same fact is made equally prominent in the account of the next great conversion of Philippi, which in its general circumstances was as different as possible. When the terrified jailer asked the question, "What must I do to be saved?" the answer was, "Believe on the Lord Jesus Christ, and thou shalt be saved, *and thy house:*" and the history proceeds to say that "*he and all his*" were baptized, and that he "rejoiced, believing in God with *all his house.*" I need not proceed further, or I might adduce "the household of Stephanas" at Corinth,[1] and other instances. What I desire to urge is this, that Christian life in the Church is based on Christian life in the Family; that within our homes is the mainspring of that machinery which benefits society at large, and that in this history of the foundation of the European Church are lessons, to every one of us, of commonplace domestic duties.

(7.) One other brief remark concludes all that is possible here, in illustration of the conversion of Lydia, considered as an example to our own times and to ourselves. When she received the Gospel into her heart, she immediately supplied *help* to the *Ministers* of that Gospel. She gave them a home. She furnished them with a starting-point for their work. She promoted that union with kindred spirits which furthers the good progress of Religion. When she and her household had been baptized, St. Luke adds: "She besought us, saying, If ye have

[1] 1 Cor. i. 16.

judged me to be faithful to the Lord, come into my house, and abide there: and she constrained us."

Not that they were unwilling; but the narrative is so given as to bring out prominently to view, not only her humility, but her zeal, and her determination to show her gratitude by doing good. And there is another verse at the end of the chapter which might pass unobserved, but which it is very important to notice in this connection. After Paul and Silas had suffered "shameful" treatment at Philippi,[1] — their bodies lacerated with rods, their limbs tortured in the rack, — on being set free, we read that "they went out of the prison, and entered into the house of Lydia," and there "saw the brethren."[2] This shows that her service had not been the result of a mere fitful impulse, but that she had given them continuous help; that they were at home in her house, and that they could confidently count on her effectual aid in promoting the work to which they were devoted. Lydia is certainly worthy of high honor as the first in Europe who gave a home to the Ministers of the Gospel, and as the precursor of all those who, by endowments, by subscriptions, by sympathy, by coöperation, have made their ministrations easier and more effective than they would otherwise have been, and more commensurate with the wants of the world.

This remark would bring us, by an easy transition, from the simple example of Lydia into the

[1] 1 Thess. ii. 2. [2] Acts xvi. 40.

midst of those great church questions which happily are the subjects of eager debate just now: such as the part which lay people ought to take in church-work; the best way of organizing the religious services of women; the various methods of securing and increasing resources for spreading the Gospel at home and abroad. I say it is a happy circumstance that these subjects are eagerly debated. For debate leads to improvement, and diversity of opinion is far better than indifference.

But into such matters we cannot enter now. We may just recur to one remark which was made at the outset concerning the cheerfulness which characterized this early introduction of Christianity into Europe. It is a very bright place in the history of the world; and it is always good policy to dwell on anything that is cheerful, and to make the most of it. Prosperity does not last long. It would not be good for us if it did. Prosperity does not last long in the Church. And doubtless a long absence of trouble would not be good for the Church. At Philippi the clouds came very soon over that bright sky, as we see when we leave this quiet scene by the river side to pursue the history.

And yet there is even a permanent cheerfulness connected with the Church of that place. Read the letter written afterwards by St. Paul to that Church. No other Epistle is so free from blame. He calls the Philippians his "joy and his crown."[1] He

[1] Phil. iv. 1.

speaks with gratitude of their faithfulness and generosity. And in harmony with all this he tells them to be happy. "Rejoice in the Lord alway: and again I say, Rejoice."[1] Compare this with the modest beginning which has been before our attention. Does not the comparison encourage us to hope that even our small efforts may lead to some permanent good? If we begin with prayer; if we are diligent in the use of appointed means; if we refer everything to God's grace; if we "study to be quiet";[2] if we are attentive to home duties; if we help those who are laboring for Christ, — then, beyond any doubt, we are bearing fruit unto God, and "our fruit will remain."[3]

[1] Phil. iv. 4. [2] 1 Thess. iv. 11. [3] John xv. 16.

III.

ST. LUKE.

"Luke, the beloved Physician." — Col. iv. 14.

THE preceding paper, in the course of some remarks on the cheerful aspect which was worn by Christianity on its transition from Asia to Europe, called attention to the fact that at this moment St. Luke was enrolled among St. Paul's companions. We ascertain this beyond the reach of doubt by the change of a pronoun. In describing the journey from Galatia — where the Apostle had been detained by sickness [1] — to the sea-coast at Troas — where he received his summons into Macedonia — the narrative uses the word "*they*" of the missionary party.[2] But on the departure from Troas the phraseology is changed, and St. Luke says, "Immediately *we* endeavored to go into Macedonia." [3] The same language, too, is continued in the narrative of what took place at Philippi. Thus far, then, St. Luke is very pointedly associated in Holy Scripture with this neighborhood.

But again, we lose sight of this mode of expression from the time when St. Paul quits Macedonia on this particular missionary circuit, and we do not dis-

[1] Gal. iv. 13. [2] Acts xvi. 6. [3] Acts xvi. 10.

cern any further trace of it till, on the next missionary circuit, several years afterwards, we find him in this region once more. His visits to Thessalonica, Athens, and Corinth, on the former journey, and his visit to Ephesus on the latter, have been recorded. Then follows a brief notice of a visit to Greece, and of a return eastwards through Macedonia. Here it is that suddenly we detect the presence of St. Luke in the same neighborhood and in the same way as before, by the change of a pronoun. "These, going before, tarried for *us* at Troas: and *we* sailed away from Philippi and came unto them to Troas."[1]

From this time he appears to have been in close companionship with the Apostle till the end of the events which are recorded in the Acts. He certainly went with him to Rome.[2] And now we have to observe further, in Epistles written during the first imprisonment in that city, that "Luke, the fellow-laborer," "Luke, the beloved physician," are among those who send salutations to Philemon and the Colossians.[3] In the Epistle to the Philippians, which was written during the same imprisonment, no such salutation is sent by him; but there is a high probability that this Epistle was written later than the others; and this leads to the presumption that the "true yokefellow," who is instructed to "help those women which labored with Paul in the Gospel," is no other than St. Luke, who may be pre-

[1] Acts xx. 5, 6. [2] Acts xxviii. 16.
[3] Philem. 24 ; Col. iv. 14.

sumed to have returned to Macedonia.[1] Thus, again, we associate him with the neighborhood of Philippi, and possibly with Lydia, who furnished the subject for our last meditation. Hence, in every way, this appears a very natural and suitable position for turning our thoughts to St. Luke.

The subject would be very large, if we were to take into account all the characteristics of his Gospel, as well as the contents, the style, and the special value of the Acts of the Apostles. Tradition, too, has been busy with St. Luke, and in a full account of him it could hardly be disregarded. It is evidently necessary to narrow our view within a small compass, bearing carefully in mind also that we are considering him in the light of one of St. Paul's companions.

Tradition says that St. Luke was a painter. This opinion rests on no true foundation; it is, moreover, comparatively modern; and it has been the fruitful source of many superstitions. And yet in one sense it is most true that he was a painter.[2] In the Book of the Acts, besides many minor portraits, we have a full-length picture of the Great Apostle of the Gentiles. We ought ever gratefully to remember how much all the ages owe to St. Luke for this. Without his aid we could not have fully known St. Paul. The portrait, too, is drawn, not merely by the hand of a master, but by the hand of a friend. St. Luke knew

[1] Phil. iv. 3.

[2] See De Pressensé, *Les Trois Premiers Siècles*, vol. ii. p. 10.

St. Paul by familiar companionship; and it is quite evident that his attachment to him was most devoted and warm. We see how thoroughly the biographer — though in one sense he is writing an autobiography at the same time — sinks and forgets himself. Thus indirectly he tells us something of his own character. In what he says of St. Paul, and in what he abstains from saying about himself, he reveals to us both his ardent and steady friendship, and, at the same time, his modesty and humility.

But much more is made known to us concerning St. Luke through what is said of him by St. Paul. He speaks of him, as we have seen, not merely as his "fellow-laborer," but also as "the beloved physician." There is more meaning in the latter phrase than appears at first sight; and we shall do well to take it as the thread to guide us, from this point, in our present reflections.

The mere fact that his profession and occupation in life are specified is full of interest. There are only two other such cases in the record which we have of the companions of our Apostle. "Demetrius, the silversmith,"[1] though his conduct had much to do with a very important passage of St. Paul's career, can hardly be said to have been one of his companions; and of "Alexander the coppersmith," or "Zenas the lawyer,"[2] we know too little to be justified in building anything on the mention of their names. Lydia, "the seller of purple,"[3] was proba-

[1] Acts xix. 24. [2] 2 Tim. iv. 14; Tit. iii. 13. [3] Acts xvi. 14.

bly brought to Philippi, and thus within the sacred circle of Apostolic companionship, by the exigencies of her trade; while of Aquila and Priscilla, who were "tent-makers," we are distinctly told that Paul "abode with them, because he was of the same craft."[1] Similarly, we are quite justified in believing that St. Luke's professional life was the occasion of his coming into close contact with St. Paul. The mere specifying of his profession in the salutation implies a great deal. It must be remembered, too, that physicians were men of high culture, and that this would establish an easy link of connection with one who, besides other great qualifications for his work, was a man of literary culture. But there is a strong probability, as was hinted in the last essay, that a deeper union between the two men subsisted than any which would be supplied by mere community of intellectual tastes. St. Paul had been suffering from serious illness in Galatia,[2] and very soon afterwards St. Luke appears with him, side by side, at Troas. During subsequent years they were frequently associated together in the closest manner; and we have the best reasons for believing that the Apostle's health was always delicate. What so natural as to suppose that the first acquaintance at Troas was marked by the exercise of St. Luke's professional skill, and that the same skill was on many subsequent occasions available for the alleviation of suffering and fatigue? How entirely this explains

[1] Acts xviii. 3. [2] Gal. iv. 13.

the peculiar warmth and definiteness of the allusion in the Epistle to the Colossians! We must carefully observe, too, that it is not merely St. Luke's medical knowledge which St. Paul mentions, but that he calls him "beloved" in connection with this characteristic. There seems to be evidently here the sense of personal gratitude for benefits received.

Proceeding now from this train of thought, it is natural to attempt to trace out some indications in St. Luke's writings of the fact that he was a physician. This can be done here only in the slightest manner; but the task will not be difficult.

It is no fancy which detects in St. Luke's Gospel the traces of a professional feeling in various incidental passages, as well as in allusions to subjects which may be properly called medical. Thus it is in this Gospel alone, in the record of that first sermon at Nazareth, that we find the prominent mention of the "healing" of both mind and body as a characteristic of the Saviour's mission; and here only, at the close of that sermon, have we the quoting of that pointed proverb, "Physician, heal thyself."[1] With this may be classed a phrase which is unique in this Gospel, in the account of what took place soon afterwards, — "The power of the Lord was present to heal them."[2] So again, we have, twice repeated, in this Gospel, a peculiar phrase having reference to recovery from sickness: "There went virtue out of Him and healed them all;" "Somebody hath touched me; for I per-

[1] Luke iv. 18, 23. [2] Luke v. 17.

ceive that virtue is gone out of me."[1] But, above all, we must notice (if we may, without irreverence, use such an expression) what is almost an amusing corroboration of the view which has been expressed concerning the existence of this professional feeling in St. Luke's Gospel. In the account which another Evangelist gives of the woman healed by the way, it is said that "she had suffered many things of many physicians, and had spent all that she had, and was nothing bettered, but rather grew worse,"[2] so that a reflection seems to be thrown on the skill of the physicians; whereas St. Luke states the fact simply thus: "She had spent all her living upon physicians, neither could be healed of any,"[3] thus casting no imputation on the skill of those who belonged to his own profession.[4]

Similarly we trace indications of the physician's mind in the mention of technical details and in the use of appropriate medical terms. To elucidate this fully, it would be necessary to compare St. Luke's Greek in these cases with the terminology of Greek writers on medical science. It may suffice to give a few illustrations. Two are furnished by the account of the healing of Peter's wife's mother. When St. Luke describes the fever as a "great" fever, and speaks of Jesus as "standing over" the patient, he is really using — as can be proved by reference to the

1 Luke vi. 19; viii. 46. 2 Mark v. 26.
3 Luke viii. 43.
4 See Smith of Jordanhill, *Diss. on the Gospels*, p. 291.

proper authors — technical forms of expression; while still by the words, "He rebuked the fever," he is careful to mark the miraculous nature of the cure.[1] The Acts of the Apostles may supply our other examples; and it is important to show that the characteristic, which is now under consideration, is common to both books. In the account of miracles of healing, the writer of the Acts has an evident tendency to dwell on symptoms; and this is a true mark of the medical mind. Thus, in relating the case of the lame man at the Temple gate, it is not merely the fact of the recovery which is stated, but it is said that "the feet and ankle bones received strength;" and it is added further, as if to mark the stages of the recovery, that "he stood and walked."[2] So the stages of the blindness of Elymas at Paphos are indicated, and the symptoms of the case, as well as the mere fact of the loss of sight, when it is said that, on the utterance of St. Paul's stern anathema, "there fell on him a mist and a darkness, and he went about seeking some to lead him by the hand."[3] The last instance may be furnished by the record of St. Paul's stay in Malta, after the shipwreck. A miraculous cure was worked there on the father of Publius, "the chief man of the island," who was suffering from dysentery in an aggravated form; and the language which St. Luke applies to the patient is as exact and appropriate as if he himself had been called in to treat the case professionally.[4]

[1] Luke iv. 38, 39.
[2] Acts iii. 7, 8.
[3] Acts xiii. 11.
[4] Acts xxviii. 8.

The Collect for St. Luke's Day is one of the most beautiful in the Prayer-book. The very form of the petition — "May it please thee" — has a soothing sound, which gives to the whole prayer a character of its own. But the main feature of the Collect is that it lays hold of that fact concerning St. Luke, which has been dwelt on above, and turns it to a spiritual use; that it sets before us this Evangelist and historian as a "physician of the soul," and offers up the supplication that "by the wholesome medicines of the doctrine delivered by him all the diseases of our souls may be healed." We could hardly occupy the remainder of our space more suitably or more usefully, than by briefly considering how St. Luke's writings may truly and distinctively be viewed as medicine for the soul. Of course, his writings have several characteristics of their own. Here the view must be narrowed to those particulars which may justly be termed medicinal and remedial for sorrow and sin. I believe those who are suffering deeply from sorrow or sin do often find in St. Luke's Gospel a special consolation. The purpose of these remarks is to suggest a probable reason.

The Lord's Prayer, as given in St. Matthew, speaks of *debts:* in St. Luke it speaks of *sins.*[1] This may serve to indicate, in a pointed way, one of the differences between the two Gospels. The characteristic Parables of the Pharisee and Publican, and of the Prodigal Son, will at once occur to the mind in con-

[1] Matt. vi. 12; Luke xi. 4.

nection with this subject. Again, while St. Matthew's Gospel always leads the mind up to the establishment of Christ's kingdom, St. Luke's Gospel diffuses itself, as it were, over the whole range of the needs of humanity. This general statement can be justified by a reference to two distinctive particulars.

This Gospel penetrates, as has often been remarked, with peculiar closeness into our domestic life; it also makes special mention of the poor, and special mention of children. All this sympathetic tendency may be summed up in a brief compass by noting how St. Luke is led to give a prominent place to widows, and to enlist our feelings on their behalf. Here only does any notice occur of that "widow of fourscore and four years," Anna, of the tribe of Aser, "which departed not from the Temple, but served God with fastings and prayers night and day."[1] Here only have we that touching allusion to the most pathetic part of Elijah's career: "I tell you of a truth, many widows were in Israel in the days of Elias, when great famine was throughout the land; but unto none of them was Elias sent, save unto Sarepta, a city of Sidon, unto a woman that was a widow."[2] Above all, it is in this Gospel only that we have the miracle at the gate of Nain; and in regard to that occurrence it is to be observed, not merely that she, whose son was restored to her from the bier, was "a widow," but that it was her "only son," and that the Lord arrested the funeral procession, because He had "com-

[1] Luke ii. 36, 37. [2] Luke iv. 25, 26.

passion."[1] By such assurances of Divine sympathy, the Evangelist, like the good Samaritan in his own parable, "pours oil and wine" into our wounds. Who can hesitate to say that a biography of Christ which presents the distinguishing features, here most slightly sketched out, is full of healing medicine for the sorrows of human life?

With the subject just considered above we might naturally associate that parable in St. Luke's Gospel, and in his Gospel only, which exhibits to us a widow seeking in vain for justice from an unjust judge.[2] But it will be best to use it for the purpose of illustrating our second point; and indeed with this end in view, we can combine it, not less naturally, with another parable, which also is found only in this Gospel. A traveller at midnight is in need of refreshment after his journey, and though at first he is rudely and selfishly repulsed, at length importunity wins the granting of the request,[3] just as, at length, the widow obtains her desire by incessant asking. A peculiar kind of parable is, in fact, given by St. Luke to persuade us that persevering prayer must be granted. The argument is, that if importunity succeeds with bad and selfish men, it must succeed with the good and merciful God.

And this characteristic of the Gospel is in harmony with what we read throughout its pages concerning Prayer. The effect on the mind is very great, when we trace out patiently in these pages all the instances

[1] Luke vii. 12, 13. [2] Luke xviii. 3. [3] Luke xi. 8.

in which our Lord invites us to the habit of prayer by his own holy example. At his baptism He was "praying" when "the heaven was opened and the Holy Ghost descended upon Him."[1] When the record is given of some of his early miracles, "great multitudes coming together to hear and to be healed of their infirmities," it is added that "He withdrew Himself into the wilderness, and prayed."[2] And as at the close of his own wonder-working, so, before the appointment of those who were to do wonders in his name, "it came to pass in those days, that He went out into a mountain to pray, and continued all night in prayer to God; and when it was day He called unto Him his disciples, and of them He chose twelve."[3] Just before his transfiguration He had gone "up into a mountain to pray;" and it was "as He prayed" that the fashion of his countenance was altered, and that his garment became white and glistering.[4] It was after He had been "praying," that, at the instance of his disciples, He gave them the Lord's Prayer, proceeding to enforce it by the parable of the Midnight Traveller, and by the argument which has been adduced above.[5] And we may conclude this remarkable catalogue by the words addressed to St. Peter at the time of the Passion. Nothing could more clearly indicate a constant habit of prayer, or more solemnly inculcate on us the duty of forming this habit, than the reference to the ter-

[1] Luke iii 21, 22. [2] Luke v. 15, 16. [3] Luke vi. 12, 13. [4] Luke ix. 28, 29. [5] Luke xi. 1.

rible "sifting" which all the disciples were destined to experience, with the addition, "I have prayed for thee; and when thou art converted, strengthen thy brethren."[1] Nor could we find anywhere a more "wholesome medicine," in all times of sin and weakness and temptation, than in these passages concerning prayer, which St. Luke's Gospel contains for us. If in other places the "doctrine delivered by him" is soothing and consoling in sorrow, these passages are medicinal and remedial for the worst "diseases of the soul."

But now, though St. Luke's Gospel comes very close to those who are suffering under sorrow and sin, it is by no means sombre or depressing in its character. On the contrary, it is marked by peculiar cheerfulness. I believe that any one, taking a Concordance into his hand, and examining the words that are expressive of joy and exultation, might test this satisfactorily for himself. It is, again, in this Gospel only that those jubilant hymns are found which mark our Lord's Nativity, and have obtained a permanent place in our Church Services. Such cheerful encouragement may well be classed among the remedies which our souls need for thorough spiritual health.

Perhaps, however, we shall conclude the subject more fitly by turning to the Acts of the Apostles for specimens of the encouraging nature of St. Luke's writing; and all the more, because we thus observe

[1] Luke xxii. 31, 32.

him again in the character of a companion of St. Paul. There is certainly no lack of tenderness and pathos in this later "treatise." It would be difficult to find anywhere a passage more touching, more expressive of deep sorrow and suffering, than the address to the Ephesian elders at Miletus. Again, as to Prayer, this is brought before us on two occasions in the most emphatic manner — incidentally, too, through St. Paul's example, as in "the former treatise" through the example of his Master — both when the Apostle "kneeled down and prayed with them all" on the shore at Miletus after that address;[1] and again at the close of the voyage, when they "kneeled down on the shore and prayed" at Tyre.[2] All that is involved in such descriptions is truly medicinal to the soul. But for the full convalescence of the soul, if the comparison may be carried so far, there is needed also the "wholesome doctrine" of warm encouragement: and this is certainly supplied in the Acts of the Apostles.

The whole tone and tenor of the book has this tendency. The cheering and strengthening communications to St. Paul — as when it was said to him in Corinth at a troublous time, "Be not afraid, but speak, and hold not thy peace: for I am with thee, and no man shall set on thee to hurt thee;"[3] or when the assurance came in the castle at Jerusalem, "Be of good cheer, Paul; for as thou hast testified of me here, so must thou bear witness also at

[1] Acts xx. 36. [2] Acts xxi. 5. [3] Acts xviii. 9, 10.

Rome;"[1] or on board the ship, in the midst of the raging storm, when he was enabled to exhort the crew to "be of good cheer," through the confidence given to himself, "Fear not, Paul; lo! God hath given thee all them that sail with thee"[2] — such cheering and strengthening communications to him ought not to be without their effect on us. And yet perhaps even more hope, with a greater trust in God's good providence, is derived to us, in our daily trials, from some of the more commonplace encouragements in this narrative: as when we find, at the beginning of the voyage to Rome, that "Julius courteously entreated Paul at Sidon, and gave him liberty to go unto his friends to refresh himself;"[3] or when, at the close of the voyage, he was greeted by the brethren, who "came to meet him at Appii Forum and the Three Taverns, whom when Paul saw, he thanked God and took courage."[4] At these times, too, St. Luke was with him, to watch over his health, and to cheer him with companionship. So we return to the topic from which our meditations began — "Luke, the beloved physician" — faithful and assiduous in all these journeys — faithful also to the very end: for we find him with the Apostle not only in the first Roman imprisonment, during which the Epistle to the Colossians was written, but in the last imprisonment of all, when others had forsaken him, and he writes with deep feeling, "Only Luke is with me."[5]

[1] Acts xxiii. 11. [2] Acts xxvii. 22, 24. [3] Acts xxvii. 3. [4] Acts xxviii. 15. [5] 2 Tim. iv. 11.

It now remains, as a consequence of what has here been elucidated, that we should thankfully discharge two duties, one having reference to ourselves, the other to those around us. The remedial power of those parts of Holy Scripture, which St. Luke was inspired to write, should be drawn into our hearts; and having made it our own, we should endeavor to dispense it, as God may enable us, for the healing of the diseases of a sick world.

IV.

APOLLOS.

"An eloquent man, and mighty in the Scriptures."—ACTS xviii. 24.

AS we pursue the course of St. Paul's biography, we see his character and work on very various sides; and, as we might naturally expect, his Companions reflect this variety. In estimating his powers of active administration, for instance, we consider him in reference to such men as Timotheus and Titus. His warm personal friendship is illustrated by Barnabas and Epaphroditus. Or, again, his influence on the mind of his Heathen associates may be in some degree appreciated by what we read of his contact with Felix and Julius. The subject of our present thoughts reminds us of another side of this varied and unceasing activity. Apollos brings us within the sphere of theology and controversy, and shows us St. Paul in his contact with religious party, and in his mode of dealing with it: whilst in studying this relation between the two men we shall certainly find copious instruction for our own times, and for each one among ourselves.

Apollos was, for a while at least, in close communication with St. Paul, and himself played no inconsiderable part in one of the great Churches which the

VIEW FROM MARS HILL.

Apostle founded. Our information on these points, and on the character of Apollos, is derived almost entirely from the Acts of the Apostles and from the First Epistle to the Corinthians. There is indeed a slight allusion to him in one of the latest Epistles; but it is too casual to furnish in itself any materials for our description and understanding of the man, though, if added to what we obtain elsewhere, it forms a fit termination to our thoughts on the subject.

The passage from the Acts of the Apostles may be given at length. "A certain Jew, named Apollos, born at Alexandria, an eloquent man, and mighty in the Scriptures, came to Ephesus. This man was instructed in the way of the Lord; and, being fervent in the Spirit, he spake and taught diligently the things of the Lord, knowing only the baptism of John. And he began to speak boldly in the synagogue: whom when Aquila and Priscilla had heard, they took him unto them, and expounded unto him the way of God more perfectly. And when he was disposed to pass into Achaia, the brethren wrote, exhorting the disciples to receive him: who, when he was come, helped them much which had believed through grace: for he mightily convinced the Jews, and that publicly, showing by the Scriptures that Jesus was Christ."[1] Now here several things come to view which ought to be well considered when we wish to appreciate fully the work and the character of Apollos.

The first thing to be taken into account in estimat-

[1] Acts xviii. 24–28.

ing any man who has played an important part in life is the influence to which he was exposed in his early days. The associations of his youth; the place of his training; the manner of his education, — these things have usually much to do with the career which follows.

Now we know what Alexandria was. Even in the Acts of the Apostles we see it in its relations to the religious life of the Jews in Jerusalem,[1] and to the world-wide commerce of Heathen Italy.[2] This city was a most remarkable meeting-place of East and West, and was characterized alike by mercantile and mental activity. Even the memory of Alexander, its great founder, would tend to produce breadth of view among the Alexandrians, to make them tolerant and less disposed than others to lay stress on national distinctions. Here too the Hebrew Scriptures were translated into Greek; and here a famous school of Biblical interpretation grew up side by side with schools of Greek philosophy. Such mutual relations of Jews and Gentiles in this place were among the providential preparations for the spread of Christianity. In the midst of these influences Apollos was brought up; and the accomplishments thus acquired were of essential service to him in his future work. Even if we consider Alexandria only as a school of high education, a resort of learned men, and a place affording opportunities, if rightly used, for the training of the mind, it is instructive to observe how God made

1 Acts vi. 9. 2 Acts xxvii. 6; xviii. 11.

use of such opportunities in preparing his servant for his appointed task. And this thought leads us to the homely but very useful remark, that we ought to set a high value on early training, even as regards this world's studies. We cannot tell to what beneficial and religious purposes a good education may be made subservient.

Another thought, too, is suggested by thus viewing Alexandria as the starting-point of one of St. Paul's Companions. It is interesting to mark how God draws from different sources what is meant ultimately to flow together in one beneficent stream. The contrast between St. Paul's training and that of Apollos was probably very great. The latter was nurtured in Greek scholarship at Alexandria. The former was "brought up" in Rabbinical learning "at the feet of Gamaliel" in Jerusalem.[1] Yet afterwards they met, and became fellow-workers in the cause of the Gospel. It is an example full of instruction and encouragement to ourselves, inviting us, in regard to our own experience and our own coöperation with others, to consider and admire God's providential ordering of the early steps of our lives.

Hitherto we have been looking rather on the secular side — now we must turn to the more directly religious side — of the preparation of Apollos for the work that was appointed him. And this we see comprised in two particulars. First, we find, as indeed we should expect from the circumstances of the case,

[1] Acts xxii. 3.

that he was learned in the Old Testament Scriptures. Next we are told that he had received some instruction — only elementary, it is true, but still very important — in the facts and doctrines of Christianity.

We cannot dwell too carefully on this, that it was through being "mighty in the Scriptures" that Apollos became mighty in other respects. This knowledge of the Jewish Bible, this apprehension of its meaning, this power of explaining and illustrating its contents, became the basis of all his subsequent usefulness. It requires the exercise of but little thought to draw out all the benefit of this example for ourselves. With him this sacred possession was limited to the Old Testament. We have, in addition, the still higher blessing of the New. So that whatever argument there was in his case for the acquisition of rich stores of Biblical knowledge is immensely strengthened in ours.

But, though the Scriptures, with which Apollos was familiar, were simply the books of the Old Testament, he had obtained, before he came to Ephesus, some knowledge — and good knowledge, too, though imperfect — of the Christian Revelation. He had been "instructed in the way of the Lord," so as to be able to "teach diligently the things of the Lord," knowing, however, only the baptism of John. Whether he had come in contact with John the Baptist personally, or acquired his knowledge through some of those who had heard John's preaching in Judæa, and who had gone from thence to Alexandria, we cannot tell. The latter supposition is the more probable. However this may be, he knew the Gospel system up to the level of John's teaching, and no higher.

Now here a remark may be made, which is worthy of some attention. If Apollos knew all that John the Baptist had taught, he knew the most important part of Christianity; for John had said of Jesus, "Behold the Lamb of God, which taketh away the sin of the world." [1] The Gospel system, indeed, contains much more than this. In due time Sacraments were instituted; a Ministry was set apart; a great system of Morals was given, applicable to all the circumstances of our lives; above all, the teaching and strengthening power of the Holy Ghost was made known and promised.[2] But in these words of John the Baptist by the bank of Jordan we have the main point. This is the life-giving part of the Gospel system. However far our religious attainments may ultimately reach, it is here — in the Redemption wrought out by Christ for sin — that we have the fresh well-spring from which all the rest flows out. Let us never lose this thought from our mind. In all our study, in all our work, let the great central principle never be overlaid or forgotten.

But now we begin to enter upon considerations which relate not so much to the advantages and opportunities that Apollos possessed, as to features of his personal character.

[1] John i. 29. [2] See Acts xix. 2, 3.

It is said here that he was "eloquent." Now on this I do not dwell, except so far as to note that God chooses His instruments suitably. Eloquence is a gift bestowed only on a few. We may be very useful without eloquence. We may be very mischievous with eloquence. The point of real moment to all of us here is, that in the case of Apollos this gift was sanctified and turned to a religious use.

A similar remark, too, might perhaps, with justice, be made regarding his "fervency of spirit." Apollos was evidently a man of warm temperament; and temperaments vary. Some are naturally warmer than others. And yet is it not evident that there must be warmth wherever the true love of Christ is present? There must be enthusiasm where Christ has been received fully into the heart; and enthusiasm in ourselves is God's instrument for kindling enthusiasm in others. So that in this respect, too, there is something for every one of us to learn from Apollos, and to make the ground-work of self-examination.

But the same sentence presents to us another feature, which might not at first sight attract our notice. "This man was instructed in the way of the Lord;" "he taught diligently the things of the Lord;" he learnt the way of God "more perfectly." From these phrases, especially as read in the original Greek, I should infer that he had that habit of mind which we call accuracy; and it is a most important habit — far more important than is commonly supposed. The difference between one man and another in regard to real influence in the world relates not so much to amount of knowledge as accuracy of knowledge. Moreover, progressive advance in religious knowledge depends, at each step, upon accuracy. And now we ask the further question: On what does accuracy depend? The answer is easy. For the most part it depends on attention. An inattentive learner never becomes an accurate scholar. Justly then do we lay great stress on attention, in the teaching of the young. The exercise, too, of this faculty depends in a great measure upon ourselves; so that here again Apollos is brought face to face with our own experience, and gives to us in his example a most useful admonition.

But at this point — in the mode of his coming in contact with Aquila and Priscilla, and so indirectly with St. Paul — we begin to note a moral and religious feature of Apollos, which merits our special attention, because it is singularly characteristic of him, as well as full of beneficial suggestions to ourselves. When Aquila and Priscilla had heard Apollos in the synagogue, " they took him unto them and expounded unto him the way of God more perfectly." These two Jewish Christians, as we learn from the early part of the chapter,[1] were " tent-makers," with whom St. Paul had made acquaintance at Corinth, and whom he had left at Ephesus a short time previous to the arrival of Apollos. They became the religious

1 Acts xviii. 3.

instructors of this Alexandrian stranger, who in their hands was a most willing learner. Thus here we have an eloquent man, a learned man, a fervent man, not unwilling to be taught, and taught too by plain and homely people, who were engaged in business. One of these teachers, moreover, was a woman. It was not from a Theological College that Apollos obtained his advanced religious instruction. In making this observation we are certainly not justified in suggesting that Scripture throws any contempt on learning or scholarship. We have seen the very contrary above, in the cases both of this Jew of Alexandria and of St. Paul himself. Still the fact is as stated here. The secular training of Apollos came from a very distinguished source, his high religious training from a very lowly one. How frequently has this been the case since! Those who have been eminent in University honors have often learnt their best lessons of religion even from the poor, and often from women, in the retired hours of domestic life. By such methods God's Providence brings all parts of a man's experience into harmony, and causes all to bear upon the one point of active service. Those men who produce great religious results on the minds of others have usually drawn their own teaching from very various sources. Many things are made tributary to that stream of wide influence, which in the end flows full and strong. There must, however, be a teachable spirit, if the benefits are to be fully realized. We must become children, if we are to be high in the kingdom of heaven. This was exemplified in the instance of Apollos. Let it be our honest desire that it may be exemplified in ours.

Next we turn to notice the active career of usefulness on which he now entered. Equipped, as we have seen, with varied knowledge, he was filled with a noble zeal to make that knowledge fruitful. His desires turned with characteristic energy to a distant scene of labor; nor is it difficult to conjecture the reasons which attracted his thoughts towards Corinth. The name and importance of the place were very familiar to him. Alexandria, Ephesus, and Corinth were connected together by the intercourse of constant trade. But especially his friends Aquila and Priscilla would, in their conversation, be constantly speaking of St. Paul's work in Achaia, where they first had met him. The names of his chief converts, too, would be frequently mentioned, with the difficulties and troubles of the young Christian community in that district. Thus Apollos was seized with the desire of doing public service on the field which was prepared to his hand, and of continuing the work which St. Paul had already begun; and Aquila and Priscilla were in nowise loth to encourage him in the enterprise. They evidently rejoiced in the prospect of such aid being given to their Corinthian friends, whom they knew to be in the midst of perilous temptations. "The brethren" in Ephesus shared these feelings, "and wrote, exhorting the disciples to receive" Apollos. The mention of this fact is full of interest, for it is the first recorded instance of commendatory letters, — a kind of correspondence which became, in the times that immediately succeeded, an instrument of the utmost value for binding together the separated parts of the growing Church. Armed with such letters, Apollos crossed the sea from Ephesus to Corinth; and the result is told in forcible though simple language: "When he was come to Corinth, he helped them much which had believed through grace; for he mightily convinced the Jews, and that publicly, showing by the Scriptures that Jesus was Christ."

What a great position was this, and what an enviable position, to be the organ of friendly communication between two Churches, to bind together two parts of the Christian community, and to communicate strength where strength was needed! And let it not be forgotten that helping work of this kind, on a smaller or larger scale, is within the power of us all.

Here it is that we see the exertions of St. Paul and Apollos in the cause of the Gospel, though starting from two different points, brought harmoniously into one focus. Attempts indeed were made, too successfully, to separate the Church of Corinth into antagonistic sections, connected with the names of these two men. But in heart and intention their work was one. Just at this moment of St. Paul's life it is that the First Epistle to the Corinthians comes in, to enable us to continue the biography of Apollos, and to obtain from it fresh lessons very useful for our times.

The Epistle, soon after its opening, makes very pointed allusions to Apollos. After introductory salutations, thanksgiving, and advice, the Apostle begins his rebuke suddenly: "It hath been declared unto me of you, my brethren, by them which are of the house of Chloe, that there are contentions among you. Now this I say, that every one of you saith, I am of Paul; and I of Apollos; and I of Cephas; and I of Christ;"[1] and, again, after an interval, he returns to the same subject thus: "Whereas there is among you envying, and strife, and divisions, are ye not carnal, and walk as men? For while one saith, I am of Paul; and another, I am of Apollos; are ye not carnal? Who then is Paul, and who is Apollos, but ministers by whom ye believed, even as the Lord gave to every man? I have planted, Apollos watered; but God gave the increase."[2] At this point it is worth while to notice in passing how exactly yet how unconsciously, so to speak, the facts here implied harmonize with the history which we find in the Acts. The Corinthians are reminded that Apollos continued among them the work which Paul had begun. Paul arrived first at Corinth, Apollos afterwards. But this is not all. It is implied that Apollos had been there in the interval between St. Paul's personal visit on the Second Missionary Journey, and the writing of this letter, which we know to have taken place at Ephesus on the Third Missionary Journey.[3] It is not, however, any corroborations of

[1] 1 Cor. i. 11, 12.

[2] 1 Cor. iii. 3-6.

[3] See Acts xix. 1; 1 Cor. xvi. 8, 19.

the mere accuracy of Scripture, however interesting they may be, to which our attention is to be turned at present. We are following the career of one of St. Paul's Companions, with the view of learning from his life and work something useful for ourselves.

The arrival of this learned and eloquent man, though intended for the spreading and deepening of practical religion, had been followed, as we see, by the formation of religious parties. Some of these Corinthian Christians had a preference for St. Paul, some for Apollos. So they ranged themselves in different sections, and called themselves by different names. All this was very natural, though very wrong. Each of these two Missionaries of Christ had his own peculiar gifts and means of influence. In all that we usually sum up under the term popularity Apollos was probably far superior. On the other hand, St. Paul had been first in the field, had founded the Church in Corinth, and came with supreme authority. Besides this, individual hearts and minds had been relatively brought more closely into contact with the one or the other. Thus that deplorable growth of party spirit took place at Corinth, which has had its counterpart ever since in all ages of the Church, which is bearing its mischievous fruits even now, too plentifully, in England.

It is not needful here to attempt any discrimination of the exact characteristics of these parties in Corinth; nor indeed is this an easy task. It is more important for us to ascertain the cure for this evil tendency among ourselves. The true remedy is to be found in those general principles which St. Paul enunciates in this Epistle. We are to look up to that one common Divine source from whence all gifts and graces proceed. He reminds the Corinthians that they are to think even of their greatest teachers — whether they were Apollos or Paul himself — as "ministers" through whom God works in them spiritual good. They are not to exalt one at the expense of another. They are to view all the spiritual benefit that comes to them by human instrumentality as sent by God. "Let no man glory in men," he says; "for all things are yours — whether Paul or Apollos, or things present, or things to come — all are yours."[1]

Now the question arises — and in estimating his character it is quite essential to answer the question — whether this party spirit, which was developed at Corinth, was in any way the fault of Apollos, and whether, when it was developed, he encouraged it at all. Here another passage from the latter part of the same Epistle presents itself to our attention, and supplies the answer. The Apostle writes: "As touching our brother Apollos, I greatly desired him to come unto you with the brethren; but his will was not at all to come at this time; but he will come when he shall have convenient time."[2] We perceive from this that Apollos had now left Corinth and

[1] 1 Cor. iii. 21, 22. [2] 1 Cor. xvi. 12.

returned to Ephesus, and that he and St. Paul were in personal companionship together. It is the first record which we possess of their actual meeting, though indirectly, as we have seen, they had been in diligent coöperation. At Ephesus they had abundant opportunity of conversing together concerning the state of things in Corinth; and, viewed in the light of this fact, the verse before us is very instructive. There is no doubt that, with so much zeal, so much learning, so much eloquence, so much popularity, Apollos might have made himself eminent as a party leader. In most ages of the Church such gifts have been used, too willingly, for such purposes. But this Apollos would not do. There are good reasons, as we have seen, for believing that in some attractive qualities he was far superior to St. Paul. But he preferred the safety and welfare of the Church to his own self-aggrandizement. And how considerate is his conduct, as made known to us on this occasion! St. Paul wished him to go to Corinth at this time. But for the present he firmly declined. His appearance there would only have been the signal for a new outbreak of this party spirit.

And indeed how admirable is the conduct of these two apostolic men one towards another! We are considering them as Companions; and their mutual relation, with the personal feeling exhibited on each side at a critical time, must be specially observed. Nor is there any difficulty in seeing, on the part of St. Paul, the greatest generosity, with the most perfect confidence that Apollos would not abuse an opportunity; and, on the other side, the most delicate and thoughtful respect for St. Paul, and the utmost reluctance on the part of Apollos to run any risk of exalting himself at the expense of another. What an example of self-restraint and mutual consideration is presented to us here! Such an example ought to be carefully followed. It is this kind of forbearance which maintains and strengthens friendship, and secures the continuance of associated Christian work.

Friendships thus cemented last long and bear many strains. We are not surprised by the anxiety shown by St. Paul long afterwards for the comfort of Apollos in the prospect of a fatiguing journey. In his Epistle to Titus we find this message: "Bring Zenas the lawyer and Apollos on their journey diligently, that nothing be wanting unto them."[1] Of Zenas we know nothing, but of Apollos we know much; and we might reasonably conjecture from this passage that he and the Apostle had been brought into continually nearer companionship, and that they had often travelled together. In itself, as was remarked at the outset, it is too casual to give us much information; but it is in harmony with, and a fitting conclusion to, all the rest.

This meditation on the life and work of Apollos, imperfect as it is, may at least serve as an illustration of the large amount of religious instruction which we may secure to ourselves from the study of a Scripture

1 Titus iii. 13.

Character. Recognition of God's hand in our early training, a good and conscientious use of opportunities, a ready zeal for Christ's service, humility in learning from those who are further advanced in the Christian course than ourselves, a cheerful rendering of timely help to those around us, a firm discountenancing of factious party spirit, a considerate care for the reputation and comfort of others; can we not all, through the Holy Spirit's aid, form such habits of mind as these? The example of Apollos is not above the standard at which we ought to aim. Sometimes the characters of Scripture seem to be far removed from our own experience, and almost to belong to another world. Not so here. The pattern is quite on our own level, and singularly suitable for our own times.

This is just the kind of life which, if we are true Christians, we must desire to lead. And we may revert, as we end, to one encouraging thought to which expression was given in the earlier part of this paper. The providential guiding of Apollos in connection with St. Paul was very remarkable. His early knowledge of Christianity began at Alexandria; his mature training was received, and his active work began, at Ephesus; his distinguished public career was run at Corinth. Thus three great cities saw the three stages of his religious progress. Or we may set before our minds this fact of providential guidance in another way. St. Paul, apparently by accident, meets Aquila and Priscilla at Corinth. There, through intercourse with him, they become fitted for influence on a large scale. At Ephesus, Apollos is brought under this beneficial influence. And finally he is laboring at Corinth on the foundation laid by St. Paul, while the Apostle is again coöperating with Aquila and Priscilla in Ephesus. We may justly put all this side by side with our own experience in regard to changes of home, of occupation, of companionship; and may draw from it the comfortable assurance that, wherever we are, if we have a true desire to serve God, He will provide for us suitable work, and, so far as we need, Christian sympathy.

V.

TITUS.

"My partner and fellow-helper concerning you."—2 Cor. viii. 23.

THE word "companionship" is very far from summing up St. Paul's whole relation to those who were closely associated with him during his varied and eventful life. Of course, even his friendships are full of interest, because they illustrate features of his character and display the principles on which he acted. But each of these friendships became also the basis of coöperation. They were not merely occasions for the interchange of kindly personal feeling, but were turned into efficient helps of active and sustained work in the cause of Christ.

Nor, again, does the word "coöperation" by any means sum up all the remainder of what was involved in these relationships. In St. Paul were found a large capacity and a pressing zeal for *administration.* He used his friends without losing their affections. He sent them on suitable errands. He combined their services in fitting proportions. He posted them in places where, in his judgment, they had appropriate work to do. He corresponded with them by letter when he could not see them personally. In fact, during his short life, a considerable part of the Levant was covered with the net-work of his organization.

We might connect this organizing and governing faculty of St. Paul with various friends whose names are known to us. The most obvious of all would be Timotheus, whom we can trace through a long period in the most intimate communication with the Apostle, acting under his orders, strengthened by his sympathy, sent by him on various errands, till at last we see him placed by his authority at Ephesus, to ordain, to govern, to teach, to exercise discipline. But this eminent friend of St. Paul being above all others associated with him "as a son with his father," [1] and having labored together with him through a long range of time up to the very close of his life,[2] may with advantage be reserved for the conclusion of our series. Or, again, we might have selected Silas, who, partly in conjunction with Timotheus, became St. Paul's associate and fellow-laborer, when he separated from Barnabas;[3] but that Second Missionary Journey, to which this conjunction belongs, has already been illustrated, so far as our limits allow, by Lydia, Luke, and Apollos. Or, again, we might take for the basis of some remarks on St. Paul's administrative powers, Tychicus and Trophimus, who are prominently named as his companions on the Third Missionary Journey,[4] and who appear afterwards in close

1 Phil. ii. 22. 2 2 Tim. iv. 6, 21.

3 Acts xv. 40; xvii. 14; xviii. 5. See 1 Thess. i. 1.

4 Acts xx. iv.

communication with him: the latter in Jerusalem, in the midst of very eventful circumstances;[1] the former in connection with the sending of the Epistles to the Ephesians and Colossians during the first Roman imprisonment,[2] as well as at a still later period.[3] But on the whole they come to view less distinctively and prominently than Titus, who also suits chronologically the place at which we are now arrived, and to whom, moreover, as well as to Timotheus, a letter was addressed by the Apostle, which has both a personal and an official character, and which is preserved to us in the canonical Scriptures.

The notices of Titus in the New Testament are not very copious; but they are sufficient for our present purpose, which is to contemplate him as a specimen and sample of the Companions used by St. Paul for the spreading of truth, the promotion of charity, and the refuting of error; and perhaps our end will best be accomplished by considering, first, the general methods on which St. Paul acted as an administrator, and, secondly, certain characteristics of Titus himself, so far as they can be ascertained.

I. It is not difficult to enumerate the qualities which make a man powerful in acting on the minds and hearts of others, in using and regulating their services, and in winning and maintaining their confidence. Nor are the proofs wanting that these qualities were

1 Acts xxi. 29. See 2 Tim. iv. 20.
2 Eph. vi. 21, 22; Col. iv. 7.
3 See Tit. iii. 12; and 2 Tim. iv. 12.

combined, to a high degree of perfection, in the Apostle Paul.

The first of these qualities, which I should be disposed to specify, is the possession of *a well-understood line of policy*, and the pursuance of it with a clear vision and a strong will. Mastery over the minds of others is never obtained by those who do not know their own mind. But where a fixed end is kept distinctly in view and steadily and firmly sought, this always gives confidence to weaker natures, and supplies direction to subordinate help. When men are so led, they follow easily and instinctively. Now certainly there was never any doubt as to the tendency of St. Paul's chief thoughts and warmest feelings. The one point on which his eye was habitually fixed, and to which he turned again after every discouragement, was the securing in the hearts of all men a reception for Christ and his salvation. His speeches, his letters, his whole course of conduct, all declare this as clearly as possible.

Next to this may be mentioned *the habit of never sparing himself.* Sometimes it happens that there is latent self-indulgence in the leaders of other men. Such leadership, however, is apt to break down in the end, and at least it must fail in exciting enthusiasm. St. Paul was always ready to do more himself than he expected from others. No general with mutinous soldiers ever threw himself more heartily and personally into the work of his campaign, than did this Apostle with his army of willing and loyal followers.

At all points we find the same habit of indefatigable exertion: as at Lystra, when he rose from what appeared to be his deathblow, and turned at once to new missionary work;[1] or at Troas, when, in the midst of a fatiguing voyage, he spent the whole night in exhortation and teaching;[2] or at Miletus, when, having a few hours to spare, he sent for the Ephesian presbyters, that he might strengthen them for the discharge of their duties;[3] or in Rome, when, immediately on his arrival, he "called the chief of the Jews together," that he might "see them and speak with them concerning Christ and his salvation."[4]

But for consummate leadership other qualities are wanted, besides the clear pursuance of a settled line of policy and a ready willingness to undertake hard work. The power of *facile adaptation* is an important element in the composition of such a character; and this was eminently conspicuous in St. Paul. He could easily bend to circumstances, while keeping his main end resolutely in view and never relaxing his active exertions. If he cannot preach the Gospel in Asia, he will make the attempt in Bithynia.[5] If he refuses to circumcise Titus under conditions of one kind, he is willing to circumcise Timotheus under circumstances of another kind.[6] If he is in prison and precluded from travelling, he can write letters, and thus pursue his old work in a new way. He can

1 Acts xiv. 19–21.
2 Acts xx. 7, 11.
3 Acts xx. 15–17.
4 Acts xxviii. 17, 20.
5 Acts xvi. 7.
6 Acts xvi. 3; Gal. ii. 3.

be a Jew to the Jew — a Gentile to the Gentile — "all things to all men, that by all means he may save some."[1] Such versatility, when it is united with consistency and self-denial, is sure to win varied adherents and to retain them, whereas the stiffness of mere obstinacy repels or alienates many, whose active assistance would otherwise be willingly given.

A still deeper point of character must now be mentioned, on which the real force of administrative ability very largely depends. St. Paul had an unaffected *sympathy* with the sorrows and joys, the difficulties and successes, of those with whom he was associated. They could always reckon on his personal interest in everything that concerned them, as, on the other hand, they knew that he always took for granted a similar interest on their part in regard to all his concerns. And this mutual affection extended, not merely to progress or discouragement in the great cause of religion, but to questions of health and of minute personal comfort. It is needless to give examples to illustrate either the power of such feelings, or the fact that they had a large influence in St. Paul's administrative career. Two such instances will come before us in order, when we turn our thoughts to Onesimus and Epaphroditus.

With this deep inward affection must be united that easy habit of giving outward expression to considerate feelings, in manner, in words, in writing, which we call *courtesy*, before we have enumerated

[1] 1 Cor. ix. 22.

all St. Paul's capabilities for exercising influence on others and commanding their services. Rudeness of behavior and want of tact forfeit much coöperation, even when higher qualities are present, that deserve to retain it. St. Paul was singularly accomplished in regard to the finer points of social intercourse; and the great cause of Christianity gained much in his hands from this circumstance. We see this in his address to Agrippa, and in his letter to Philemon; nor can we doubt that his daily conduct among his companions and fellow-laborers was marked by this feature.

Our enumeration may conclude with the mention of his *discriminating judgment.* This faculty is essential for a successful leader of other men. Unless he can distinguish among their characters, so as to see what duties are best suited for each, and so as to treat them according to their several temperaments, confusions and misunderstandings must result, and the best work must be impeded and retarded. That St. Paul possessed this power of discrimination to an unusual degree is very evident. While dealing with the progress of the Gospel on the broadest scale, he had a remarkable capacity of singling out individuals for distinct observation and recollection. We see this in the specific prayers which he offered up according to the emergencies which came before his attention. We see it in the appropriate variety of the messages sent, in the course of his Epistles, to different persons. We see it, too, in the assigning to his companions separate missions, suitable to the disposition and capabilities of each. A marked instance of this is to be found by means of comparing Timotheus and Titus.

This brings us back to the point from which we started. And now, leaving these general remarks on St. Paul's administrative power, we may turn our attention to Titus, as furnishing in his career an illustration of the exercise of this power, besides affording to us in his own personal character some very useful suggestions for our conduct.

II. Most persons, reading the Epistles to Timothy and the Epistle to Titus carefully, and then comparing them, will be conscious of a difference in tone, which leads to an impression that there was a marked difference of character in the two men. This method of drawing the distinction may be somewhat fine and delicate. It does not, however, follow from this that the distinction itself is fanciful. Moreover, it bears the test of a close examination. In the Epistles to Timothy no one can fail to observe a peculiar tenderness of feeling. The allusions to the childhood of Timothy;[1] to his mother and his grandmother;[2] to his tears;[3] to his delicate health;[4] to his companionship with St. Paul in time of suffering,[5] as well as the strong injunctions not to show weakness in the discharge of his duties,[6] — lead us

[1] 2 Tim. iii. 15. [2] 2 Tim. i. 5. [3] 2 Tim. i. 4.
[4] 1 Tim. v. 23. [5] 2 Tim. iii. 10, 11.
[6] 1 Tim. i. 18; vi. 13, 14; 2 Tim. ii. 1.

to infer the existence of something like a feminine softness in the character of Timothy.[1] No such features are conspicuous in the Epistle addressed to Titus. Its tone is altogether more abrupt and severe. This may arise partly from the character of that rough Cretan population among whom the duties of Titus were to be discharged; but it is natural to connect it also with the character of Titus himself. St. Paul writes as if he did not fear any weakness on his part, and as if he expected him to be fully competent for the hard task assigned to him.

With this introductory remark, suggested by the comparison of two men whose names almost necessarily present themselves as parallel words, we may proceed to follow the Scriptural notices of Titus in their chronological order. He is not mentioned in the Acts at all. The requisite information must be derived from the Epistle to the Galatians, the Second Epistle to the Corinthians, and the Pastoral Epistles.

Our series of slight biographical notices has brought us now to the Third Missionary Journey of St. Paul. On this circuit, as on the former, the earlier part of his progress was through the district of Galatia. We have seen that on the first of these occasions he was detained there by illness, and joined soon afterwards by St. Luke. Shortly after the second visit he heard of a very rapid declension of his converts into serious errors; and this caused him to write the Epistle to the Galatians. It is here that

[1] See art. "Timotheus," in the *Dictionary of the Bible.*

the first notice of Titus occurs; and it is observable that he is mentioned in such a way as to convey the impression that he was well known to the Galatian Christians. From this we should infer that he was among St. Paul's Companions on this part of his missionary travels. Certainly he was with him, as we shall see, and in active service under his orders, very soon afterwards.

The facts mentioned in this Epistle concerning Titus carry us back to an earlier time. St. Paul, in the course of his argument on the freedom of the Church from the necessity of Jewish practices, has occasion to mention the important journey undertaken by himself and Barnabas from Antioch to Jerusalem. Among "certain others,"[1] who were with him, was Titus;[2] and it is added that "he, being a Greek, was not compelled to be circumcised."[3] Great efforts were evidently made to exercise compulsion; but they were most firmly resisted, and the resistance was enforced, as we perceive in the context, by vehement arguments. Now here we see that Titus was a true Gentile, not, like Timotheus, of half-Jewish descent.[4] He was, in fact, a representative of the Gentile Church on this occasion, as Barnabas was of the Jewish. We see also that Titus had been at Antioch with Paul and Barnabas during the time of their active and united work in that place. A very natural inference is, that he had been

[1] Acts xv. 2.
[2] Gal. ii. 1.
[3] Gal. ii. 3.
[4] Acts xvi. 1, 3.

converted then and there. In the Epistle addressed afterwards to himself he is entitled St. Paul's "own son after the common faith,"[1] which associates him with this Apostle by the closest of ties, both personal and religious. Of the occupation of Titus in the interval between this conference at Jerusalem and St. Paul's second visit to Galatia, a period of several years, we know nothing. Of the occurrence which is recorded in connection with that conference this is worth observing, that Titus appears there in connection with the firm and uncompromising side of St. Paul's character, just as the circumcision of Timotheus, on the other hand, exhibits him on the side of conciliation.

Soon after writing the Epistle to the Galatians, on this Third Missionary Journey, St. Paul had occasion to write the First Epistle to the Corinthians. This letter was elicited from him by very serious abuses affecting morality, as those in Galatia had affected doctrine. It can be shown by very satisfactory arguments[2] that Titus was one of the bearers of this letter from Ephesus to Corinth. And now again he appears in parallelism and in contrast with Timotheus. That disciple, too, was sent on a mission to Corinth about the same time. But he certainly did not take the letter. And at this point it occurs to make the observation, that the missions of the two

1 Tit. i. 4.

2 1 Cor. xvi. 11, 12. See a compact statement of the case in art. "Titus," in the *Dictionary of the Bible.*

men appear to have been very different, and in harmony with their respective dispositions. The words concerning Timotheus are: "If he come, see that he may be with you without fear; for he worketh the work of the Lord, as I also do. Let no man therefore despise him: but conduct him forth in peace, that he may come unto me; for I look for him with the brethren."[1] The impression derived from this is, not that Timotheus was a robust controversialist, but rather that he was sent on some message of conciliation. Titus, on the other hand, as one of "the brethren" who conveyed the letter, was the bearer of very stern rebukes; and this collision with the abuses at Corinth would make a considerable demand on him for firmness and decision, to say nothing of the promptitude and energy which were required about this time, as we shall see, by the business of the collection now in progress for "the poor saints in Judæa."

With the Second Epistle to the Corinthians, which followed the First at a short interval, we come upon a clear view of Titus. The materials for describing his character are no longer conjectural, or derived from minute arguments. St. Paul speaks of him and of his mission warmly and openly to the Corinthians. And, first, his intense anxiety to meet Titus on his return from Corinth, in the interval between the first and second letters, and to hear the news he brought of the Church in that place, must be made the subject of remark.

[1] 1 Cor. xvi. 10, 11.

While Titus was still absent, St. Paul proceeded from Ephesus to Troas "to preach Christ's Gospel;" and he adds that there "a door was opened to him of the Lord." Still he says he had "no rest in his spirit, because he found not Titus his brother," but "taking his leave of them, went forth from thence into Macedonia."[1] There, to his great joy, he met Titus, and received from him good intelligence respecting the converts who had made him so anxious. Nowhere in St. Paul's Epistles is a warmer expression to be found of exuberant thanksgiving and happiness; and we can see very plainly that this feeling is connected with certain personal qualifications in Titus himself. He was "filled with comfort; he was exceeding joyful in all his tribulation." On his arrival in Macedonia, "his flesh had no rest, but he was troubled on every side: without were fightings, within were fears. Nevertheless God, that comforteth those that are cast down comforted him by the coming of Titus." It was something to enjoy the sympathy of a congenial companion; but far more than this: "not by his coming only" was the Apostle comforted, "but by the consolation wherewith Titus had been comforted in the Corinthians." He was able to tell the Apostle of their earnest repentance, of their fervent mind towards himself, of their sorrow for their sin, of their vehement indignant efforts for the clearing of themselves.[2] Now the point of interest for us here is, that Titus shared all the

[1] 2 Cor. ii. 12, 13. [2] 2 Cor. vii. 4-11.

feelings of St. Paul. Whatever joy and comfort the Apostle experienced in the recovery of these erring Corinthians was reflected, and, indeed had been anticipated, in the messenger. It was not simply St. Paul that was "comforted by the consolation;" but Titus, who brought the news, also felt the consolation. And all this is brought to view below still more explicitly: "We were comforted in your comfort; yea, and exceedingly the more joyed we for the joy of Titus, because his spirit was refreshed by you all. His inward affection is more abundant towards you, whilst he remembereth the obedience of you all, how with fear and trembling you received him."[1] Nothing could display more clearly, both the affectionate and loyal nature of Titus, and also his thorough abhorrence of evil, and hearty rejoicing in the truth.

But this is not all that the Epistle before us enables us to ascertain in regard to the mission and the character of Titus. The question of the collection, in which St. Paul took so warm an interest, was involved in some embarrassment at Corinth. In this place there had evidently been much profession of alacrity at first, and some considerable abatement of zeal afterwards. It is very possible that the party spirit, which had grown up to so disastrous a height in this Church, had produced its usual injurious effect on practical works of charity. However this might be, the messenger, who was authorized to deal

[1] 2 Cor. vii. 13, 15.

with this question, was required to have firmness and tact, as well as strict integrity; and, in both respects, Titus receives the strongest testimony from the Apostle. As to the latter point, while indignantly repelling an imputation which had been cast on his own honor and unselfishness, he says, "Did I make a gain of you by any of them whom I sent unto you? Did Titus make a gain of you? Walked we not in the same spirit? walked we not in the same steps?"[1] As to the former, we have the utmost commendation both of the zeal he showed in animating them at the outset, and of his moral courage afterwards in kindling their flagging generosity.[2] The sentences which are used on this subject by the Apostle imply the existence in Titus of very high qualities, which, added to what has been mentioned above, show him to have been a character well worthy to be admired and imitated. The mere fact of his being sent on such a mission is high praise; and nothing can exceed the confidence expressed in the words, "Whether any do inquire of Titus, he is my partner and fellow-helper concerning you."[3]

Again there is a considerable space, during which his biography is a blank. Titus does not appear in companionship with St. Paul on any subsequent journey; nor does his name occur in connection with any event at Jerusalem, or the imprisonment in Rome. Neither is this the place for inquiring and deciding where and at what time the Epistle to Titus him-

[1] 2 Cor. xii. 17, 18. [2] 2 Cor. viii. 6, 16, 17. [3] 2 Cor. viii. 23.

self was written. The general strain of the letter has been spoken of above, as affording some insight into the characteristic disposition and ability of Titus. The Cretans, among whom he is placed, are described in most unfavorable terms ;[1] and under these circumstances, he is to " set in order the things that are wanting," to " exhort and convince gainsayers," to " stop the mouths of unruly and vain talkers," to " rebuke sharply," to " speak the things that become sound doctrine," to " show himself a pattern of good works," to preach " obedience to magistrates," to " reject heretics."[2] He to whom such a commission was confidently intrusted by St. Paul, could not have been wanting in energy, firmness, judgment, and force of character.

One sentence in this Epistle forms an apparent link of connection with the latest notice of the name of Titus. St. Paul says to him: " Be diligent to come unto me to Nicopolis : for I have determined there to winter."[3] Now we find it stated in the last of the Pastoral Epistles, written shortly before St. Paul's death, that " Titus was gone to Dalmatia."[4] This was a wild and rugged district, with a rough population, not far from Nicopolis ; and there may have been some connection between the two journeys. Neither tradition nor history helps us to any details. It is just worth while to observe, that this mention of a difficult mission and an inclement season is in har-

[1] Tit. i. 12. [2] Tit. i. 5, 9, 11, 13; ii. 1, 7; iii. 1, 10.
[3] Tit. iii. 12. [4] 2 Tim. iv. 10.

mony with the temperament and capabilities of Titus and the work which the Apostle was in the habit of assigning to him.

It is, however, with the island of Crete that this companion of St. Paul must be closely and permanently associated. And such an association is well adapted to attract the imagination and to fix itself in the memory. The commanding geographical position of *Candia*, in advance, of the Archipelago, and in the line of seafarers on their voyages from Syria to Italy; the grand outline and solid masses of its mountains; the fame of its mythological traditions; the hereditary turbulence of its inhabitants; the rough vicissitudes of its history, — combine to make it memorable among islands. The Biblical student, too, can never forget that one of the most remarkable passages in St. Paul's history was connected with its southern coast.[1] Nor has the memory of Titus, in the midst of many superstitions, ever been lost in the island. When the Venetians occupied it, they gave to " St. Titus " a place side by side with their own " St. Mark." We may conclude with an extract from a panegyric pronounced by one of his successors in the episcopal superintendence of Crete. Andreas Cretensis says that Titus " laid the foundation of the Church in Crete, was himself there the pillar of the Truth and the strong support of the Faith, the unwearied trumpet of the proclamation of the Gospel, and the clear utterance of the tongue of St. Paul."

[1] Acts xxvii. 7–16. See art. " Crete," in the *Dictionary of the Bible.*

VI.

PHŒBE.

"A succorer of many, and of myself also." —ROM. xvi. 2.

IN the second of these papers, when attention was turned to the first coming of Christianity with St. Paul into Europe, and to the Scripture notices of Lydia, as illustrating the methods by which the Gospel made progress on its new field, some remarks were made on the religious service of women as apparently characteristic of the Church in Philippi.[1] The scope of these remarks might very easily and justly have been extended; and we have now reached a point where it ought to be extended. It may be said with perfect truth that the religious service of women is characteristic of Christianity itself, and that we see this most clearly in connection with St. Paul and his Companions.

That the Gospel has raised woman to a higher point than any which she ever occupied before, we all admit. Not only is this seen to be true on comparing the Christian world with all parts and all ages of the Heathen world; but it is found to be true too when we institute a careful comparison between Christianity and Judaism. In reading the Old Tes-

[1] Acts xvi. 14, 15, 40; Phil. iv. 2, 3.

tament and the New we are conscious of a difference between the two, in regard to the relative part played by women, though it may not be easy to express this consciousness in definite words. For the sake of marking the contrast, so far as this can be done in a single sentence, let us take the case of the widow. Who is so much honored now as the Christian widow? What a respectful recognition we pay to her sorrow and her experience! What a great place she has in the Christian Church, for influence, for advice, for the promotion of good works. Such is the spirit in which she is spoken of in the New Testament.[1] But it is not exactly so in the Old. The tone in which she is mentioned there is different. There she is rather the object of compassion; and if we turn, beyond the pages of Scripture, to other early Jewish writings, they seem to place her almost in a position of contempt. This may suffice as a glance at a mere corner of a large subject, namely, the elevation of women through the coming of Him, who, Himself, "born of woman"[2] has left with them henceforward a peculiar power of efficient ministration.

Such ministrations began even in the earliest Gospel days, during the sojourn of our Saviour on earth. In fact all the great principles of Christian Life and the Christian Church, and this principle among the rest, were foreshadowed in the records of that Biog-

1 See especially St. Luke's Gospel (ii. 37; iv. 25; vii. 12; xviii. 3), with Acts vi. 1; ix. 39, and 1 Tim. v. 9.

2 Gal. iv. 4.

raphy. We may omit, if we will, the mention of Anna, the pious prophetess "of the tribe of Aser," as belonging rather to the end of the Old Dispensation than the beginning of the New;[1] and also of St. Mary, the mother of our Lord, "and her cousin Elizabeth," as standing apart in a sphere of their own.[2] But when we turn beyond the period of Christ's infancy and youth, to the beginning of his active work, we find him punctually aided by the devoted sympathy and service of women. They followed Him from place to place; they practiced self-denial for his sake; they found their happiness in diminishing his toil and supplying his wants. When St Luke describes our Lord as "going throughout every city and village, preaching and showing the glad tidings of the kingdom of God," he proceeds to say not merely that "the twelve were with him," but likewise "certain women." Then three are specified; and it is added that there were "many others," who, with those three, "ministered to him of their substance."[3] This was in Galilee, the scene of numerous journeys and of much active work. From thence some of them—"many of them"—followed him into Judæa, at a time when the Apostles were full of fear;[4] and still the description given of them at the Cross is that they were "ministering."[5] They held themselves in readiness to do anything that they might be able to do for Christ; and this waiting in readiness is most truly the

[1] Luke ii. 36-38. [2] Luke i. 5-58. [3] Luke viii. 1-3. [4] Mark xv. 41. [5] Matt. xxvii. 55.

spirit of serving. From the Cross to the Grave they "followed" Him still,[1] and even at the Grave itself we see in them the same spirit of serving. It might have been supposed when the great stone was placed at the door of the sepulchre, and when evening came on, that all occasion, all possibility, of "ministering" was over. But such was not the view of these women. When they went away from the sepulchre, it was still to do Him honor. They bought and prepared sweet spices for the embalmment of the body.[2] Can we fail to see in this an anticipation and prophecy of that feminine service which became a distinguishing mark of the Christian Church?

If we turn to the Book of Acts, with the illustrations of it supplied by the Epistles, we find this service appearing in a more systematic form. As regards the women mentioned above, even they are seen once more, just after the Ascension, in company with the Apostles.[3] And when they are lost to view, others of the same sex become prominent in efficient ministrations. We need not lay undue stress on the "widows" to whom our attention is turned in the account of the appointment of the first deacons,[4] or on the "widows" who surrounded Dorcas;[5] though in both cases we seem to perceive the germs of the organization of charity. It is of course, as has been said, in connection with the life of St. Paul that we should expect the fullest notices of such feminine

[1] Luke xxiii. 55. [2] Mark xvi. 1. [3] Acts i. 14. [4] Acts vi. 1. [5] Acts ix 39, 41.

ministrations as were characteristic of the earliest Church.

With St. Paul everything takes a wider range; and we begin now to see more clearly the place which women are destined to occupy in relation to the social life of Christendom. Lydia has already furnished occasion for some remarks at length. Priscilla, with her husband, will be the subject of one of these papers, before the series is closed. But besides these, other women are mentioned in the Acts, though in a slight, yet in a significant way. Damaris [1] might fairly be adduced as an example of bold confession of the faith, such as women have often made, when men have faltered. The daughters of Philip,[2] who had the gift of prophecy, can hardly be thought to have resided as unmarried women in their father's house, without doing useful service to the Church. But when we turn to the Epistles, we find a profuse number of instances, which tend to prove our point. Chloe [3] and Appia,[4] Euodia and Syntyche,[5] are mentioned by name among the women who were directly or indirectly associated with St. Paul in promoting the cause of the Gospel at places as widely separated as Corinth, Colossæ, and Philippi. And especially it is in the Epistle to the Romans that we find a catalogue of female names which almost startles us, when we think of the early period to which this document belongs. The salutations in the sixteenth chapter, in-

[1] Acts xvii. 34. [2] Acts xxi. 9. [3] 1 Cor. i. 11.
[4] Philemon 2. [5] Phil. iv. 2.

cidental as they are, give us much information as to the facts of the case. The number of female fellow-workers, who are mentioned there by name, and with a distinct reference to their Christian coöperation, is remarkable. Priscilla appears here, as elsewhere; and we find, among other women, the following specified also, with an allusion to their service: "Mary, who bestowed much labor on us;" "Tryphena and Tryphosa, who labor in the Lord;" "Persis, which labored much in the Lord."[1] Such phrases imply a system of wide-spread sympathy and service in the Christian cause.

It is, however, in the name and description of Phœbe that the whole case is most completely summed up. As regards both her direct association with St. Paul, and the exact account of her character and work, she must always demand our special attention in connection with this general subject. St. Paul says, at the beginning of this sixteenth chapter: "I commend unto you Phœbe our sister, which is a servant (a deaconess) of the church which is at Cenchreæ; that ye receive her in the Lord, as becometh saints, and that ye assist her in whatsoever business she hath need of you: for she hath been a succorer of many, and of myself also." Each of the particulars named in these verses may be made the subject of a few remarks in order.

(1.) We may, in the first instance, pause with advantage on the name of the place with which the

[1] Rom. xvi. 6, 12.

name of Phœbe is thus connected in the Epistle to the Romans. *Cenchreæ*, from whence she came, was the eastern seaport of Corinth, and distant from that city about nine miles. Corinth was as remarkable in its situation as memorable in its history; and every part of St. Paul's connection with its neighborhood is full of interest. He was twice there. His first visit was on the Second Missionary Circuit; on his return from which we find him sailing from this very harbor of Cenchreæ.[1] The second residence at Corinth was in the Third Missionary Circuit; during which he wrote the Epistle to the Romans. It is not unlikely that he wrote the letter immediately before his return to the East; and it is almost certain that Phœbe conveyed it. Thus, on both occasions, the Apostle is very definitely associated with Cenchreæ; and in the mention of "the church that was at" this place, we seem to have an indication of a rapid and wide-spread advance of Christianity at the Isthmus. It may be inferred, that in connection with the central church in Corinth there were organized suburban churches, with their systematic agencies for charitable and religious work.

(2.) An official position is evidently indicated by the statement that Phœbe was a "*servant of*" a local church. She was clearly no mere volunteer, acting outside of all ecclesiastical arrangements. This, however, is not the place for discussing the charitable and religious ministry of women on its

[1] Acts xviii. 18.

strictly ecclesiastical side: it is enough to make a remark, in passing, on its importance. What is passing in nearly all parts of Protestant Christendom, including the United States of America, makes it evident that a new sense of the urgency of this question has grown up in many minds. It is felt that we require something more in this direction than we have been accustomed to possess since the Reformation. "Nothing, indeed, could be more undesirable than that charitable work should be regarded as the employment of a distinct and professional class, instead of being the duty of the whole Church, and therefore of each member of it, according to the opportunities presented in his or her course of life. But it is precisely work of this kind which has led to the recognition of the fact, that there are forms of evil and suffering with which it is unable to cope, which demand the complete devotion of time and strength from those who are able to give it.[1] And it is certainly a fact of some moment that we find the woman-deacon,[2] as well as the man-deacon, in the Apostolic Church, and thus possess all the sanction which we require for what is felt to be very needful in the Modern Church.

(3.) We pass on to the account which is given of

[1] Preface to the *Life of Pastor Fliedner* (translated by Catherine Winkworth), p. xviii. It is truly said (p. vi.) that this story "places before us a courageous and hard-working life, concentrated with unusual constancy and good sense on one aim, and achieving it with rare success."

[2] This is the true meaning of 1 Tim. iii. 11.

Phœbe's past services. She had been "*a succorer* of many." This phrase is very beautiful: and, even in the English, it means a great deal. Yet it fails to express the whole sense of the original. "Succor" may be given in various ways; but the term here employed would seem to indicate one who had stood forth as the patroness of the unprotected and despised. There is no doubt that the Christians were objects of contempt at this time in Achaia; and even if this were not the case, the Greek word would in itself imply moral courage, generous bounty, and large sympathy; and the points of importance to us here are that these qualities are exhibited by a woman, and in such a way as to promote the progress and strength of the New Religion. There seems good reason for supposing that Phœbe was a person of some rank and substance. We might place her in comparison with the "great woman" of Shunem, dwelling "among her own people," who showed hospitality to Elisha; and certainly the Apostle's feeling finds expression in language very similar in tone to that used by the Prophet: "Behold, thou hast been careful for us with all this care; what is to be done for thee?"[1] There is this interest too in the comparison, that one of these scenes is eminently characteristic of the Old Testament, the other eminently characteristic of the New. The state of society in the Greek cities of the Levant, during St. Paul's day, was of such a kind as to give peculiar emphasis to

[1] 2 Kings iv. 8, 13.

the attitude taken by Phœbe. Nor was her help afforded merely to St. Paul. She had been a succorer of "*many.*" A large amount of brave and active service is revealed to us in this phrase. Phœbe is a worthy follower of the women of the Gospels, and a useful example to all those of her sex who desire to employ fully the special power which God has given them for promoting the cause of Christ.

(4.) But St. Paul adds: "*and of myself also.*" Here we encounter that warm personal feeling, which gives so great a charm to St. Paul's intercourse with his friends, whether recorded in the narrative of the Acts, or exhibited in his letters. Gratitude is one of the marked features of his character; and the manifestations of it break out at every turn. He remembers how affectionately the Galatians received him, when he "preached the Gospel to them at the first." [1] He remembers how generously the Philippians aided him "in the beginning of the Gospel" on the European continent, by sending him funds to Thessalonica.[2] In writing to the Colossians, he specifies those who were "a comfort to him." [3] In writing to Timotheus, he mentions Onesiphorus, who "oft refreshed him, sought him out in prison, and was not ashamed of his chain." [4] Even this very chapter which furnishes our present contribution to the series of St. Paul's Companions, has several instances of the same kind. Aquila and Priscilla are stated to have "laid

[1] Gal. iv. 13–15.
[2] Phil. iv. 15, 16.
[3] Col. iv. 11.
[4] 2 Tim. i. 16–18.

down their necks for his sake." Mary has "bestowed much labor on him." Urban has been "his helper." Gaius has been "his host." Thus it is with regard to Phœbe. It is no mere formal and official errand on which she goes to Rome; but he follows her with his gratitude. The letter which she carries is a record of what he owes to her; and this obligation is made the ground of an appeal to the Roman Christians, to enforce the duty of their receiving her with confidence and respect, and of aiding her to the utmost of their power.

(5.) This brings us to our last point. The Christians are to "*receive* Phœbe *in the Lord, as becometh saints*," and to "*assist* her in whatsoever business she hath need." Each of these clauses merits a separate and careful attention. "In the Lord" is a customary phrase with St. Paul. It denotes in such a passage as this community of interest under Christ, and points to the fact that all the persons in question, and all their concerns, belong to Him. But it means even more than this. It suggests the thought of coöperation in the same kind of religious work. We might compare what is said here to the Romans of Phœbe with what is said to the Corinthians of Timotheus:[1] "If he come, see that he may be with you without fear; for he worketh the work of the Lord, as I also do;" or with what is said to the Philippians of Epaphroditus:[2] "Receive him in the Lord with all gladness; and hold such in reputation: because for

[1] 1 Cor. xvi. 10.

[2] Phil. ii. 29, 30.

the work of Christ he was nigh unto death." As to the phrase, " worthy of the saints," it may be difficult to decide whether the meaning is that Phœbe is to be received in such a manner as she herself deserves, or in such a manner as would be a matter of course with the Roman Christians if they were what they professed to be. We may be quite content to leave this point indeterminate, and to consider that the phrase includes both meanings. But, further, they were not only to give her a friendly and worthy reception, but to furnish her with all the assistance she needed for the errands on which she was sent. Such a request was clearly most reasonable. St. Paul is here asking help for one who herself had been a helper of " many." We must add the additional claim arising from her venturing on the risk and toil of a long voyage by sea, which was then a far more formidable undertaking than it is now.

Here the remark may be made, that if Phœbe is herself an example and a pattern, this injunction to the Romans is equally an injunction to Christian people of all times, that they give aid to those who honestly follow in her steps. When women are earnestly devoting their lives to the service of Christ, in active exertion and generous self-sacrifice, they ought to be helped and reinforced by sympathy and respect, and by " whatsoever they have need of " to make their work effectual. Better than all mere church-organization is this free and willing help; and, indeed, without such help, organization is very apt to degenerate into dead machinery.

But whilst urging the peculiar claims of faithful feminine service on the respect, assistance, and encouragement of the Christian community at large, we must not forget that there is another side of the subject which closely and seriously concerns a great number, perhaps the greater number, of the readers of this paper. If Christianity owes much to women, let it be recollected how much women owe to Christianity. We have seen above how they have been elevated, and what new powers they have received, through the coming of Christ. They ought then unceasingly to bear in mind the corresponding demand which this fact has established upon them for devotion and service. They cannot be too forcibly reminded that thenceforward there rests on them a peculiar responsibility, a peculiar call to gratitude and to enthusiasm for Christ. Let them not fall below the position in which He has placed them. Let them cast aside their besetting temptations, and do the work which it is appointed to them to do — remembering the women in Judæa and in Galilee, at the Cross and at the Grave — remembering also the women who aided the Apostles, and, in what has been well called the "private ministry of the Word," became the best missionaries of domestic life.

There is good reason too why men, especially in these uneasy times of ours, should keep well in mind the peculiar benediction which rests on godly women, and their peculiar aptitude for efficient service under the Gospel. We ought to recognize those special capabilities; we ought to make the most of them, and devise methodical plans for that end by the exercise of our best wisdom. No effort could be more in harmony with the will of Christ and the practice of his Apostles. Jesus Christ accepted the ministry of the Galilæan women; and the Apostle of Jesus Christ has messages of special earnestness and significance for the "women which labored with him in the Gospel."[1]

[1] Phil. iv. 3.

VII.

FELIX.

"And Felix, willing to show the Jews a pleasure, left Paul bound." — Acts xxiv. 27.

THE earliest points of contact between Christianity and Heathenism must of necessity possess for us a permanent interest, and may be expected to supply us with instruction of peculiar value. In our own day, indeed, Christianity has its points of contact with Heathenism; and each such instance is full of interest for every serious mind, and full of instruction even for us at home. This is found to be the case by all who care to study with attention the modern records of Missionary progress. But we must expect to find a peculiar freshness and a forcible reality in all instances of this kind which are recorded in Scripture concerning that time when Christianity was new, and when Heathenism was only beginning to be dislodged from its ancient strongholds.

Such points of contact are, of course, mainly to be found in the history of the life of that Apostle who was especially designated to the office of evangelizing the Gentiles. Undoubtedly we must not forget Cornelius, whose conversion in one sense overshadowed all other Gentile conversions. But still St. Peter, when he had thus opened wide the doors of the Universal Church, fell back into the position of the Apostle of the Jews, and, as regards the heathen world, made way for St. Paul.

Four marked instances of contact with Heathenism in connection with his life, as recorded in the Acts, will at once recur to the reader's memory, — two having reference to Heathenism in its rude and uncivilized form; two bringing before us states of society where both culture and business had reached a high standard. The two former are the scenes at Lystra, where the people first sought to worship St. Paul as a god, and then endeavored to stone him to death;[1] and at Melita, when the process was inverted, and when, after supposing him to be a murderer, they said that he was a god.[2] Here we see Christianity face to face with ignorance, superstition, prejudice, and fanaticism. The other two are the discourse on Mars' Hill at Athens,[3] and the tumult among the silversmiths at Ephesus.[4] Here we see how the Gospel of Christ is called to encounter both the sneers of supercilious philosophy and the unscrupulous intrigues of self-interest. And still, is it not too true that our Holy Religion has the same enemies to meet, — ignorance, superstition, self-conceit, selfishness, — and that not only in the heathen world outside, but at home among ourselves?

These four instances, however, show to us the con-

1 Acts xiv. 11–19.
2 Acts xxviii. 2–6.
3 Acts xvii. 22.
4 Acts xix. 24.

tact of Christianity with Heathenism on the great scale, and in reference to general truths with their opposing errors. We may expect to obtain instruction for ourselves, still more pointedly and directly, through such contact with the individual consciences of heathen men. In observing what moral phenomena are exhibited on such occasions — in seeing how St. Paul, on the one hand, deals with such persons; and how, on the other hand, they act under his influence, receiving the truth, or resisting it — we are prepared to find that principles of great importance come to view, with permanent admonition or encouragement for our own conduct. There are various such instances in St. Paul's life. Such names as those of Sergius Paulus, of Gallio, Claudius Lysias, and Festus, will at once occur to us.[1] I select, however, those two which seem to me the best, partly because they represent, more than any others, a close personal intimacy with St. Paul, and partly because they are very different in character from one another. I take Felix the Governor for my present subject, and for our next subject I propose Julius the Centurion.

We are to examine the character of Felix, the manner in which the Gospel was presented to him by St. Paul, and the manner in which he acted when God providentially granted him this great opportunity. In order to appreciate these things no long introduction will be necessary.

Felix was the Roman Governor of Judæa, and re-

[1] Acts xiii. 7; xviii. 12; xxiii. 26; xxiv. 27.

sided, as was the custom, not in Jerusalem, but in the government-house at Cæsarea on the coast. The Apostle was first brought face to face with him when he was conveyed to this place as a prisoner from Jerusalem. On his return from that visit to Greece, during which we last saw him sending Phœbe with the Epistle to the Romans, he had been violently attacked by a Jewish mob in the Temple court;[1] and Claudius Lysias, with some soldiers from the garrison, had rescued him, but was much perplexed by the case, besides becoming aware of a conspiracy among the Jews to take away his life.[2] Accordingly he sent him, under a strong escort, to Cæsarea with a letter to the Governor; and the twenty-third chapter ends with these words: "When they came to Cæsarea, and delivered the Epistle to the Governor, they presented Paul also before him; and when the Governor had read the letter, he asked of what province the prisoner was," and having ascertained this, he said to him, "I will hear thee when thine accusers are also come."[3]

In this there was evidently nothing to blame. Felix acted like a clear-sighted man of business, and apparently with a due sense of the responsibility of office. So far our first impression is favorable. But as we pursue the narrative we begin to see beneath the surface. And here the remark is suggested, that we must not judge of men by their public official

1 Acts xxi. 31, 32. 2 Acts xxiii. 12, 21, 23.
3 Acts xxiii. 33-35.

appearances. A bad man may be a very equitable magistrate. Nor are lay people only to be included within a sentence which invites to serious self-examination. A clergyman too may preach well and forcibly — may discharge his general clerical duties in a very faultless manner — while yet he is not truly in his heart a religious man. This example of Felix — even at the first glance — is full of searching and penetrating questions for every one of us.

On the trial which took place at Cæsarea, when Tertullus, who held a brief for the Jews, made an ingenious and complimentary speech, and St. Paul made an honest and manly defense for himself, we need not dwell. Felix appears again at the close of the proceedings in what we must pronounce, upon the whole, a favorable aspect. "Having more perfect knowledge of that way," the narrative says, "he deferred them, and said, When Lysias the chief captain shall come down, I will know the uttermost of your matter." In these words, knowing Felix as we do from other circumstances, we can, indeed, see very clearly the working of interested motives; and we feel that he ought to have set St. Paul at liberty. Still, on looking at the matter merely by itself, it might very fairly be argued that he wished to maintain a strict observance of the Roman law, to exercise due caution, and to act fairly.

What follows, too, might be taken to indicate a kind-hearted disposition, as well as a desire to act legally and justly. "Felix commanded a centurion to keep Paul, and to let him have liberty, and that he should forbid none of his acquaintance to minister or come to him." In the case of a state prisoner like St. Paul, who was also a Roman citizen,[1] there was always the power of giving great alleviation to the imprisonment; and this power Felix freely used for his benefit. The Apostle was allowed to be comparatively "at liberty." This did not, indeed, involve so much freedom as what we call in England being allowed to go on bail. He was always under the eye of an officer of the army. Still he was not thrown into a dismal dungeon, as he had been at Philippi.[2] There was perfect freedom to see his friends, to converse with them, and to receive their help. We are well aware how great a difference this must have made to St. Paul, when we remember his sociable and loving disposition. But more than this. In thus being allowed freely to converse with "his acquaintance," he had the opportunity of prosecuting his work. Those who were Christians already would, to use his own words elsewhere, "wax confident by his bonds."[3] Those who were not Christians could see, better than they could under other circumstances, what strength and elasticity there is in the principles of the Gospel. All this suggests to our minds even a feeling of gratitude to Felix for the liberty which he accorded to our Great Apostle.

But, further, the way in which this was done seems to argue considerate care and deliberation. We have

1 Acts xvi. 37; xxii. 25. Acts xvi. 24. 3 Phil. i. 14.

evidently here the very words of the order which he gave. The centurion was not only to let Paul "have liberty," but to "forbid none of his acquaintance to minister or come to him." There is the impression here of his entertaining a favorable opinion of St. Paul, and of something like personal regard. Either the report of Claudius Lysias, or his own recent interview with the prisoner, may have produced an influence on the mind of Felix. However this may be, we see that he gave a very kind and considerate treatment to St. Paul. And at this point the remark may be permitted, that even such conduct as this is not always a true indication of character. Various inferior motives may persuade a bad and selfish man to act in such a way that he is praised and admired for his kindness. There may be in such a case the carelessness of weak good-nature; there may be the calm calculation of sagacious policy. We have no right, indeed, to assert the presence of such motives in any instance which comes in contact with our own experience in society; but sometimes other features of character come to view which force us to such a judgment — which lift the veil, and enable us to see a selfish, cowardly, unjust, time-serving man under an exterior show of benevolence and fairness. So it was in the case of Felix.

"After certain days, when Felix came with his wife Drusilla, which was a Jewess, he sent for Paul and heard him concerning the faith in Christ; and as he reasoned of righteousness, temperance, and judgment to come, Felix trembled, and answered, Go thy way for this time; when I have a convenient season, I will call for thee." Here we suddenly discover a totally different aspect of the man; and one singularly in harmony with what we know of him from other sources. We have, in fact, a great deal of independent information concerning the life and character of this Governor of Judæa. They are described to us by an eminent Jewish and an eminent Heathen historian. From these authorities we learn that he had once been a slave, and that, with his brother, he obtained his freedom and rose to power through sordid flattery and by making himself the useful instrument of the crimes of great men. When thus raised to unenviable eminence, and installed in his place of power at Cæsarea, he was cruel, unscrupulous, and mercenary. Having bought his position by base subserviency, he used it for selfish tyranny. The Heathen historian, to whom I have referred, expresses this in a terrible sentence by saying that, "in the practice of all kinds of lust and cruelty he exercised the power of a king with the temper of a slave." He was the cause of a great amount of tumult and bloodshed in Judæa; he encouraged and profited by plunder and extortion; and, as the Jewish historian tells us, he procured the murder of the High-priest, at a sacred festival, and by the hand of a friend of the High-priest himself, who had been bribed for the purpose. His private life, too, was profligate and licentious. This very woman Drusilla had been enticed from her husband by help of a fortune-teller. On the whole, the private character and public administration of Felix were so bad and exasperating, that they were spoken of among the causes which hastened on the ruin of the Jewish nation. It was before this specimen of Heathenism that St. Paul, as the representative of Christianity, now stood at Cæsarea.

This interview was not part of the Apostle's trial before Felix as Governor. It was rather a conversation than a trial; and one motive which led to the interview was clearly curiosity. Drusilla was a Jewish princess, a sister of Herod Agrippa II., who is mentioned soon afterwards in connection with Festus, the successor of Felix. It might almost seem as though idle religious curiosity was hereditary in the Herodian family. We recollect how one member of that family, at an earlier date, had, without any trace of real religious earnestness, desired to see Jesus Christ.[1] So, after this date, we find the Second Agrippa with Bernice face to face with St. Paul in a spirit not very different from that of Felix and Drusilla.[2] She must have heard of Christianity and its celebrated Apostle. The preaching and the miracles of the Gospel had not been "done in a corner." Felix seems to have shared her curiosity, or to have yielded to it; and thus it came to pass that Felix "heard Paul concerning the faith in Christ."

It is worth while to pause here, if this was one of

[1] Luke ix. 9; xxiii. 8.

[2] Acts xxv. 22.

the motives that led to the interview. There was a full opportunity of learning the whole truth of the Gospel and of becoming a Christian; but no benefit resulted. The motive was curiosity. Are there not similar instances — very many — in our own day, and with a similar absence of any beneficial result? Love of variety, love of novelty, love of excitement in matters of religion, is only a form of dissipation. Running after favorite preachers, going in crowds to attractive services, — this, in itself, has nothing whatever to do with religion in the heart. If this is all, as you come, so you go away, with only this difference, that your heart is more frivolous and more careless, because you have succeeded in coming in contact with a serious subject without carrying away any permanently serious impression.

But what did St. Paul say to Felix? *He* was really serious. *He* was really in earnest. He said nothing to gratify curiosity. His purpose was not to please, not to amuse, but, if possible, to do good. He aimed directly at the conscience. He said, not what Felix wished to know, but what it was very good for Felix to hear. He "reasoned of righteousness, temperance, and judgment." Such topics so exactly suited the case of Felix, that we might truly say that the Governor's own life and character formed the dark background on which these subjects were placed in clear relief. As to *righteousness*, he himself was acting unrighteously at this time in retaining St. Paul in prison, when no case had been proved against him. As to *temperance* or self-restraint, Drusilla was there to witness against him. As to *judgment*, Felix was about this time under accusation, and was before long summoned to take his trial in Rome. It is not, indeed, at all likely that St. Paul preached on these subjects in any rude or offensive manner. No doubt he spoke with all his usual tact, so as to win the respect of his hearers. Nor was any offense really taken. And yet the words went home. "Felix trembled." He had good reason for trembling; and he did tremble. So far an impression was made. But; after all, it was only the impression of terror on a slavish mind. As it has been quaintly expressed, "his early fears in childhood had been kept alive, and notions of punishment practically quickened, by the lashes of his master's whip," and now "he recognized his old familiar terrors, and the Gospel which could not reach him as a man, came rudely home to him as a slave, and whipped this gilded image of royalty upon his throne." [1]

Here, in passing, it is important that we should make another remark on the language used by St. Paul to Felix. "He reasoned of righteousness, temperance, and judgment to come." It might be asked, Did not St. Paul preach Christ? St. Paul always preached Christ. Who will presume to say that he ever failed in this? But we cannot preach the Gospel without preaching the Law. Unless there is a

[1] Archdeacon Evans' *Scripture Biography*, vol. i. p. 311.

sense of the Law broken, we cannot value the Gospel which heals and saves. Hence, just as at Athens, in speaking to a large number of Heathens, he said that God had "appointed a day in the which He will judge the world in righteousness," [1] so here, in addressing an individual Heathen, he uses the terrors of the Law, that he may awake the sense of sin, and the consciousness that a Saviour is needed.

"Felix trembled." But the impression did not last. He had not sought the interview with any high motive, and hence no blessing followed. He put the matter off to a "convenient season;" and, so far as we know, the impression never returned. How different was it with another eminent Roman, in this same city of Cæsarea, in the case of an interview with another Apostle! The allusion, of course, is to what was mentioned above, the history of Cornelius and St. Peter. Then all was pious, humble, and godly preparation for the truth of God. The words of Cornelius on the arrival of Peter were, "Now therefore are we all here present before God, to hear all things that are commanded thee of God." [2] Different indeed was this state of mind from that of Felix! and how different the result!

But as we come near to the end of the chapter, we obtain a further insight into the mean and contemptible character of Felix. "He hoped also that *money* should have been given him of Paul, that he might loose him; wherefore he sent for him the

[1] Acts xvii. 31. [2] Acts x. 33.

oftener, and communed with him." There could not be a greater condemnation of a magistrate. If St. Paul was wrongly imprisoned, he ought to have been set free without money. If he was rightly imprisoned, he ought to have been kept in prison, whether money was paid to the magistrate or not. Bribery was strictly forbidden by the Roman law. We see here the inveterate slavishness of the man; and we seem to see this all the more clearly, if we look still more closely into the history. It might be asked how Felix could expect such a prisoner as St. Paul to be able to find money, even if he was *willing* to give a bribe. But we find above that the Apostle told Felix in his defense, that he had come to Judæa, "to bring alms to his nation, and offerings." [1] So that he might easily imagine that St. Paul had large funds at his command. Not that these funds belonged to St. Paul. But when a man feels no scruple in practicing fraud for his own interest, he readily believes that another man will practice fraud, if *he* has something to gain by it. It is very difficult for a dishonest man to believe in the integrity of other men; very difficult for a selfish man to believe that any one will do good simply from the love of doing good.

But, to return to the words that were just now quoted, it is impossible not to wish that we could have heard the conversations of these two men. We should then have been able to appreciate the significance of that *companionship* which did in truth sub-

[1] Acts xxiv. 17.

sist between Paul and Felix. We should, indeed, then have seen Christianity and Heathenism face to face, and each with its true and full expression. This verse, however, tells us quite enough in general terms to give point to the instruction we are to obtain here. As regards St. Paul, we observe that he was quite immovable. He could probably have obtained funds from his friends for a lawful purpose without touching any money that was intrusted to him for the poor; and by means of a bribe he might easily have obtained his liberty, for he had not yet appealed to the Emperor. And, again, by so doing he would have obtained new opportunities for travelling far and wide and preaching the Gospel. But he who taught obedience to the law would not break the law, even for the purpose of saving souls.

The chapter ends with the words which are placed at the head of this paper; "After two years Portius Festus came into Felix's room; and Felix, willing to show the Jews a pleasure, left Paul bound." On this I will only remark that the contemptible and servile meanness of Felix is visible to the end. His official dignity is only skin-deep; he is still a slave. After all these conversations with St. Paul, after all these golden opportunities (golden, indeed, for such opportunities were hardly ever given to any one else in the world), he left Paul in prison, not because it was just to do so, but because he wished to have the favor of the Jews. History supplies the explanation. Felix was summoned to Rome to give an account of his conduct; and the favorable testimony of the Jews was just then of great importance to him. For this he sacrificed St. Paul, and sacrificed his own soul.

Now, as we quit the subject, one thought very naturally occurs to us. If Felix had yielded to the impression which his first interview with the Apostle of Christ had made upon him; if, when he "trembled" under the sense of his guilt and the fear of coming judgment, he had followed on to make acquaintance with the Saviour Christ, whom Paul was even then preaching to him, the result would have been very different. However seared his life was by bad and degrading habits, Divine grace could have made him a new man. But he procrastinated, and the opportunity was lost.

"When I have a convenient season, I will call for thee." This sentence suggests a very serious appeal to the reader. It may not have been "convenient" to you hitherto to begin in earnest the solemn work of saving your soul. Sin has held you in its strong grasp up to the present moment; or business has been so engrossing, that you have not been able to forget it; or a gay and giddy world has perpetually run away with all your graver thoughts. You do not indeed intend to quit this life without having secured the salvation of your soul; but you wait for a "convenient season." Now it is quite certain that you will never have a more convenient season than the present. You look forward to the beneficial results of some affliction. But what guarantee can you have that affliction will produce upon your mind the precise effect which you anticipate? Or you expect that sickness and the threatening nearness to death will convert you. But where do you obtain any promise regarding the manner of the sickness or the accident which is to be the precursor of your death? Or you wait till the attraction of those things which now absorb you ceases to be all-powerful. But how do you propose to overcome the *habits* which will have been formed under the influence of this attraction, and which will continue after the attraction has ceased? No. All such calculations are quite delusive. The vain world and your weak heart are always saying to you, like Felix, "To-morrow, not To-day." Christ says, and Reason says, and Heaven and Hell say, "To-day, not To-morrow."

VIII.

JULIUS.

"The centurion, willing to save Paul, kept them from their purpose." — ACTS xxvii. 43.

AS we study the well-defined and instructive characters which the New Testament in abundance presents to us, nothing is more remarkable than the favorable impression which the officers of the Roman army leave upon the mind. It may be that the military career is *favorable* to some attractive virtues. It may be, on the other hand, that the Scripture would remind us by these instances that eminent virtues may be formed *in spite of* adverse circumstances in the military life. We need not attempt to determine that point. Probably there is some truth in each of these suppositions; but, however we may settle that question, the above-mentioned fact is undoubted.

In the centurion at Capernaum we have the exhibition of a very high type of character well sustained throughout. He was tolerant and generous; for he built the Jews their synagogue. He was full of warm-hearted sympathy; for the illness and approaching death of his slave filled him with utter distress. His humility was remarkable; for he did not regard himself worthy to receive the Saviour under his roof.

Yet he was no weak man, but had very correct and strict notions of discipline. He recognized the obedience due to the military powers above him, and expected those beneath him to obey. "I am a man under authority," he said, "and I say to this man, Go, and he goeth, and to another, Come, and he cometh, and to my servant, Do this, and he doeth it;" and, arguing from his own position in these respects to the Saviour's power, he exhibited an example of faith which caused Jesus to "marvel." [1]

And there is another centurion in the Gospels who merits our admiration and respect. "Certainly this was a righteous man. Truly this man was the Son of God." [2] These words, spoken at the Cross, draw a sharp line of distinction between the speaker and the general company of the soldiers around. Others were mocking and blaspheming. Here was an honest yielding to conviction, and a candid confession of the truth. It is a startling fact that the first visible beneficial effect of the death of Christ was upon the mind of a soldier and a heathen; so that we recognize some force, as well as beauty, in the words of a French writer, who says, "This centurion's faith and confession are the first-fruits of the faith of the Gentiles, and the prophetic sign that the nations are now to take the place of the Jews. Jesus all his life long devoted Himself to the Jews. Instantly after his death He begins to declare Himself for the Gentiles

1 Mark viii. 10; Luke vii. 9.
2 Mark xv. 39; Luke xxiii. 47.

by this first act of grace. The first results of his death are not for a Priest, not for a Doctor of the Law, not for a Pharisee, not for any Jew, but for a Gentile and a man of war, who was simply there on military duty."[1]

Now, if we turn from the Gospels to the Book of the Acts, and examine the varied gallery of portraits which that book contains, we find there also two centurions, on whom we are constrained to look with feelings of sincere respect and warm regard.

Whatever we may say of the centurion at the Cross as a prophecy and anticipation of the bringing-in of the Gentiles, the main interest of that great change is concentrated, and intended to be concentrated, in the case of Cornelius. All the circumstances combine to draw our attention to it in the most pointed manner. That with which we are concerned here is the character of the man. It is not merely that the great act of conversion, through the instrumentality of St. Peter, is brought before us as the introduction to that blessing which is now come to all nations; but the example of Cornelius is itself a pattern. This might have been otherwise. The conversion would not have been less real, if a vile and cowardly profligate like Felix had been suddenly turned into a Christian. But it has pleased God to make Cornelius not only the sample and precursor of a great religious revolution, but also a model for our imitation. The various particulars which we learn of him can only be enu-

[1] Quesnel on Mark xv. 39, and Luke xxiii. 47.

merated here in the briefest way. But when we remember that he was a man most regular in his private prayers — that he exercised a religious influence over his household; that he was generous and liberal, and had the high esteem of the Jews who surrounded him, and that he listened most reverently and earnestly to the instructions of St. Peter; not, like Felix, when he heard the word of St. Paul, putting the matter off to a more "convenient season," — we see at once that there is quite enough to justify the strong expressions used above.[1]

St. Paul came frequently in contact with the Roman army, especially in the latter part of his career. Five centurions are mentioned in connection with the arrest at Jerusalem and the imprisonment at Cæsárea, besides those who took part in rescuing him from the mob.[2] Of course, some of them may have been the same officers, appearing at different times on different duties; and this probably was the case. But it is interesting, in connection with the train of thought with which we began, to mark these circumstances. One of these centurions was the officer — the captain, as we should say — who stood by when St. Paul was being bound with thongs, in order to be beaten, and on learning that he was a Roman citizen, informed his commanding officer — the colonel, as we should say — of the danger he was incurring.[3] The next was the centurion whom St. Paul discreetly called, when he learned from his nephew of the conspiracy

1 Acts x. 1; xi. 18. 2 Acts xxi. 32. 3 Acts xxii. 25, 26.

which had been formed against him, and whom St. Paul requested to take the young man to the commanding officer, Claudius Lysias.[1] Two others were those whom Claudius Lysias sent in command of the escort that conveyed St. Paul to Cæsarea.[2] Nothing is said to give any indication of their characters. We simply know that they discharged their duty very promptly and methodically. But when we come to the close of the imprisonment at Cæsarea, and the time of the voyage to Rome, then we meet another centurion, who quite deserves our very careful attention.[3]

Our last subject was Felix; the character now before our attention is that of Julius. Both are taken as specimens of that early contact of Christianity with Heathenism, of which the life of St. Paul furnishes the best illustrations. And, as was remarked in the preceding paper, these two men present to us this contact in two very different points of view, and with two very different kinds of instructions for ourselves.

We saw that "after two years," during which the Apostle was in detention at Cæsarea, Felix was summoned to Rome to give an account of serious charges that were made against him, and that "willing," for his own interest, "to show the Jews a pleasure, he left Paul bound." [4] Festus, who succeeded Felix, was in great perplexity in regard to this prisoner, besides

1 Acts xxiii. 17.
2 Acts xxiii. 23.
3 Acts xxvii. 1.
4 Acts xxiv. 27.

being very anxious to begin his new work without incurring unpopularity. He proposed that St. Paul should go to take his trial in Jerusalem. The Apostle saw the danger in which this would involve him; and instantly, with great tact, made use of the privilege which his Roman citizenship gave him, and appealed to the Emperor.[1] This made it necessary to send him to Rome. Some delays took place which need not be referred to here. In due time a convenient opportunity came; and, as we read in the first verse of the twenty-seventh chapter, "When it was determined that we," that is, St. Luke and St. Paul, with Aristarchus, "should sail into Italy, they delivered Paul and certain other prisoners unto one named Julius, a Centurion of Augustus' band."

The specifying of the military corps to which Julius belonged, singles him out at once as an officer of rank. He seems to have held a commission in the most distinguished part of the Roman army, and that which was the most closely connected with the Emperor and his court. For some time he had been on foreign duty at Cæsarea. Now he was about to return to head-quarters.

There are six places where he is referred to during the subsequent narrative. We will take them, very briefly, in order, with the view of learning what the Scripture teaches us concerning him.

(1.) After they set sail, "the next day they touched at Sidon;"[2] and it is added that Julius "courte-

[1] Acts xxv. 11. [2] Acts xxvii. 3.

ously entreated Paul, and gave him liberty to go unto his friends to refresh himself." Here we pause; for we have before us distinct features of the character of Julius. We must remember that he was a Heathen. This enhances the favorable impression produced on us by his courtesy and kindness. Whether this courtesy and kindness arose from his own natural disposition, or from some influence which St. Paul had already gained over him, or from what he may have observed and heard when the Apostle was brought before Festus and Agrippa (for it is highly probable that he was present on that memorable occasion), we cannot tell. In any case we admire and respect Julius for the treatment which he gave to the Apostle. We must observe that it was not a mere hard dry permission to go on shore and see his friends that was accorded. There was something, indeed, even in this. He might have insisted on his staying on board while the vessel was in the harbor. He might have said that this was the only guarantee he could have that the prisoner would not escape. Even his placing confidence in St. Paul implies a large and rapid growth of good-will between the Christian and the Heathen; and we are not surprised that St. Luke notes the circumstance. But there was a remarkable display of considerate feeling in the manner in which this was done. As it has been rather quaintly expressed by an old and well-known commentator, "Julius treated St. Paul like a scholar, a gentleman, and a friend." And then let all that is implied by two of the prominent words of this verse be considered: "Julius courteously entreated Paul, and gave him liberty to go unto his *friends* to *refresh* himself." He must have needed *refreshment* for his bodily health and for his spirits. We know that he was of a delicate constitution; and, after enduring many hardships, and going through scenes of great excitement, he had been kept "two years" a prisoner at Cæsarea, hindered from prosecuting the work on which his heart was bent, and harassed by the persecution of the Jews and the unfair dealing of the Roman governor. We all suffer from toil and excitement — from alternations between exposure to inclement weather at one time and confinement to close quarters at another — from conflict of mind and ill-treatment; nor were the Apostles any exception to this rule. And of all refreshments, the most consoling would be the congenial society of Christian *friends*. The Apostles had all our human feelings. And in St. Paul the feelings of friendship and sympathy were found in the utmost intensity. Putting all these things together, we see good reason for looking on Julius, at this point of the narrative, with admiration, respect, and gratitude.[1]

(2.) The next point at which we pause, but only for a moment, is Myra.[2] Here the centurion with his prisoners changed ships. The vessel in which

1 When Ignatius was on his voyage from Antioch to his martyrdom in Rome, the brutality of the soldiers who guarded him was such that he compared them to wild beasts.

2 Ver. 5.

they had come from Cæsarea was not going much further in the right direction; but in the harbor of Myra they found an Alexandrian vessel bound for Italy. The centurion made a bargain with the captain, and "put" his prisoners "therein." On this we need not dwell, except just to remark that Julius is expressly mentioned. All through this narrative he is the prominent person in connection with St. Paul. The new ship, as we learn afterwards, had altogether two hundred and seventy-six persons on board.[1] Our business is simply with the centurion, wherever he is mentioned, and with any features of his character that we can discover.

(3.) In this large ship they set sail from Myra, in very bad weather. The gale drove them to Crete, and they came to anchor in a roadstead on the south of that island, called Fair Havens.[2] There they stayed for some time, in the hope that the storm would abate. It would have been wise if they had stayed there longer. St. Paul recommended this course. He warned them that if they continued their voyage at that season, there would be much risk to the ship, to the cargo, and to their lives. "Nevertheless, the centurion believed the master and the owner of the ship, more than those things which were spoken by Paul." We cannot wonder at this. Any one of us, under the like circumstances, would probably have done the same; especially as, besides the master and the owner, "the more part

[1] Ver. 37. [2] Ver. 8.

advised" to leave Fair Havens. The master had experience of the sea: the owner had the best possible reasons for consulting for the safety of the ship; and there was that argument from the majority of voices which so often leads us wrong. We certainly cannot blame Julius. Perhaps we ought rather to give him credit for good sense. He could not be aware of the communications which God had made to the mind of St. Paul; and he was not in a condition to understand, or to be persuaded by, any such communications. Nor, indeed, is it certain that St. Paul spoke at this time with any prophetical or supernatural insight. Still St. Paul was right, and Julius was wrong. This came to view clearly afterwards, and was one of the circumstances which gradually raised the Apostle to a position of commanding influence over all on board. Julius apparently felt this influence above all others; and it is just worth while to remark here, in pursuing our slight biographical thread, that Julius evidently took no offense because St. Paul honestly opposed him in a debate on an important subject.

(4.) We must pass over a time of great trouble and danger, before we come to the next mention of the centurion. The gale, which overtook the ship after leaving Fair Havens, lasted a fortnight; and at the close of that period the vessel was wrecked. Before the wreck actually took place, there was a night of fearful anxiety. The ship was at anchor; but the storm was still raging, and there was the most imminent risk of her going on the rocks.[1] In

[1] Ver. 29.

these circumstances the sailors, under the pretense of doing something to anchor the ship more firmly, were preparing to lower the boat, to secure their own safety, and to leave the passengers to their fate. St. Paul understood the treacherous and cowardly design — saw the danger — but acted with consummate judgment. He said nothing to the sailors, but spoke at once to his friend the centurion and to the soldiers. He appealed, too, to their own instinct of self-preservation: "Except these" — the sailors — "abide in the ship, ye" — ye soldiers — "cannot be saved." The centurion and his men had now implicit confidence in the Apostle, and they dealt with the matter promptly. "They cut off the ropes of the boat and let her fall off." Thus the sailors were kept on board to do what was necessary — and what they alone could do — when the daylight should come: and we see how the lives of nearly three hundred people were saved through the good understanding established between Paul the Apostle and Julius the Centurion — through the contact of friendly feeling between a Christian and a Heathen.

(5.) When the daylight came, this good understanding — this friendly feeling — led, in a still more remarkable way, to similar results; and this brings us to the passage which was selected at the outset as expressing most fully the main point of the whole subject. When the vessel struck, she did not go to pieces immediately. "The fore-part stuck fast, and remained unmovable, but the hinder part was broken with the violence of the waves: and the soldiers' counsel was to kill the prisoners, lest any of them should swim out and escape: but the centurion, willing to save Paul, kept them from their purpose."[1] The advice given by the soldiers is easily understood. They were answerable with their own lives for the prisoners; and it was better for them to be able to show that they had put the prsioners to death on an emergency than to be called to account for carelessly allowing them to escape. They forgot, indeed, that they owed their own lives to St. Paul; but we cannot be surprised to find Roman soldiers selfish and cruel. And now, in this moment of imminent danger not only to St. Paul but to all his fellow-passengers, comes out conspicuously to view the peculiar feeling of Julius towards him. "The centurion, *willing to save Paul*, kept them from their purpose." Had Paul not been of the party — had Julius been a man of a different disposition — all the other prisoners would have been killed. In the end all were saved: but this was entirely due to the influence gained by St. Paul over Julius — to the friendship felt by the Heathen Centurion for the Christian Apostle.

(6.) The last mention of this centurion is in Rome itself. After the winter had been spent in Malta, another Alexandrian vessel was employed to carry on all the shipwrecked people. Nothing occurred to hinder this part of the voyage. The centurion and his prisoners landed at Puteoli — they went up to

[1] Vers. 42, 43.

Rome by the great south road — and "when they came to Rome, the centurion delivered the prisoners to the captain of the guard."[1] His duty was done. He proceeds to obey whatever new military orders are laid upon him. St. Paul is "allowed to dwell in his own hired house, with the soldier that keeps him;" and, while waiting for his trial, has opportunities of preaching the Gospel to those who come to him, and of writing Epistles to distant Churches.

A thought here occurs to the mind, which opens out into other very serious thoughts. It seems highly probable that St. Paul, Felix, and Julius were, for some considerable time, in Rome together. But, even if this was the case, it is very likely that the Apostle never met either of these two men again. A large city is like a large forest, where different paths may be pursued again and again without any chance of meeting. Each man, however, in such a city has his own history, and carries about with him the results of his past experience and opportunities. Felix was what he became after he had trembled at the reasoning of "temperance, righteousness, and judgment" — after he had procrastinated to a "convenient season" — after he had treated St. Paul unjustly, and, "to please the Jews," left him in prison. Julius was what he became after close companionship on shipboard (and where could companionship be more close?) with the Apostle — after treating him kindly — after owing his own life to him, and after saving his life in return.

[1] Acts xxviii. 16.

Whether this intercourse ripened into an acceptance of the Gospel and the new life in Christ Jesus, we do not know. But, without endeavoring to penetrate that secret, there is permanent instruction for us even in this slight biographical sketch which has been drawn by help of the last two chapters of the Acts.

What is this instruction?

We have followed the biographical thread, through a series of incidents, with very little mention of Religion. This course is in harmony with the character of the chapter itself. It is by no means one of the shortest in the book: yet no mention of Christ occurs in it from the beginning to the end. The duty of an expositor of the Bible is to deal fairly with the Sacred Volume, to take it as he finds it — to try to catch its true spirit — to study and to explain its various parts in succession — feeling sure that there is everywhere in it some Christian lesson, even where Christ is not named.

And is it not most instructive to find such variety of teaching, as we go through the parts of Scripture in order? Here we have been considering in two successive papers two of the early points of contact between Christianity and Heathenism, as exhibited in the intercourse of St. Paul with Felix and with Julius: and there could not well be a greater difference than between the impressions which these two parts of the record leave on the mind. In the one case there is the most searching appeal, in reference to the salvation of the soul, shaking the conscience to its very foundations. In the other case are the incidents of friendly intercourse, with its happy results as regards the affairs of this world. And is it not an indication of the Divinity of the Bible, that while it penetrates the depths of the soul, sets before us, in words of fire, the horrible misery of sin, and draws us, with the most intense persuasion, to the mercy of Christ, it also takes us by the hand where we are, and leads us along the path of our daily life, so that we may be happy in ourselves and a blessing to all around us?

We might say that the subject of the last essay contained warning for the unconverted, and that the subject of this paper contains advice for the converted. The instruction we are to draw from the account of this centurion relates to the duty and the advantages of *courtesy*. And let it be remembered, as was said above, that the force of the example is very much increased by the fact that Julius was a Heathen. When our Lord would inculcate the duty of active benevolence, He exhibits a Samaritan showing kindness to a wounded Jew. When we are admonished of the sin of ingratitude, we are reminded that the one man who returned thanks after the healing of the leprosy was a Samaritan. So it is here. The example of courtesy is shown on that side which the Christian mind would naturally and instinctively regard with suspicion.

We can hardly fail to read the lesson. And as to the place in Christian character which ought to be occupied by courtesy — that is, by kind consideration, polite behavior, friendly treatment — it is enough here to quote a string of texts; and perhaps it would be hardly possible to strengthen the argument derived from their simple juxtaposition. In the Sermon on the Mount we find this: "Blessed are the meek; blessed are the merciful; blessed are the peacemakers;" and also this: "Whosoever shall compel thee to go a mile, go with him twain."[1] In the First Epistle of St. Peter we find this: "Honor all men: be ye all of one mind, having compassion one of another; be pitiful, be courteous."[2] In the Epistle to the Ephesians this: "Let all bitterness and clamor be put away from you; and be ye kind one to another, tender-hearted."[3] In the Epistle to the Romans this: "Be kindly affectioned one to another with brotherly love; in honor preferring one another."[4] Whilst in the Epistle to the Philippians — written at the very period to which we are now come in our course of biographical sketches, and in the midst of those very soldiers of the Roman army, to which our attention has just been especially directed — we have the whole case summed up thus: "Let nothing be done through strife or vainglory; but in lowliness of mind let each esteem other better than themselves. Look not every man on his own things, but every man also on the things of others. Let this mind be in you, which was also in Christ Jesus."[5]

[1] Matt. v. 5, 7, 9, 41. [2] 1 Peter ii. 17; iii. 8.
[3] Eph. iv. 31, 32. [4] Rom. xii. 10. [5] Phil. ii. 3–5.

And let it not be said, in the midst of our boasted civilization, that injunctions to courtesy are obsolete. It is as needful as ever it was that the lesson should be carefully studied and well learnt; and this, too, in very various sections of our social life. Those, for instance, who have had much to do with education are well aware that rudeness in the time of boyhood is sometimes almost held as a point of honor; and it is highly desirable to point out that such behavior is not really manly, and is attended by no good consequences. Rudeness, too, both of language and manner, is still prevalent among the uneducated classes. There is no reason, however, why hands hard with labor should not accompany a perfectly gentle and polite mind; and in proportion as this change is effected, there will result a clear gain to the social comfort of life, and even to Religion.

Nor let those who regard themselves as belonging to the higher ranks of society claim any exemption from the admonition with which this subject pursues us all. There may be much discourtesy without rudeness. The presence of a certain amount of refinement may, in fact, indicate a worse violation of the Christian law, because such a state of mind contains the element of supercilious contempt. There must, indeed, be gradations in the community corresponding with varieties of employment; but the feeling which separates them in this country, if closely analyzed, would often be found to deviate far from the Gospel standard. Two young men, perhaps, have started from the same point in the career of life, and in the course of a few years one is earning his bread by the sweat of his brow, the other by some routine work of the pen: once they were companions on equal terms, but now the latter begins to look down on the former, as though belonging to an inferior race. Or two mothers, with their families, are brought into close neighborhood, and through some accidental distinction, which it is hardly possible to define, they discover that even ordinary civility is impossible. It is surely not difficult to decide that such states of feeling are out of harmony with the mind of Christ, and very injurious to the progress of his cause in the world.

Nor do such instances by any means exhaust the applications of the lesson which we have been considering. How unjustifiable, for example, are the alienations and animosities often engendered by political partisanship! and how injurious to that sacred "bond of peace" which ought to unite together all those who bear the Christian name! The vast difference between Christianity and Heathenism did not hinder the interchange of courtesy and mutual regard between Julius the Centurion and Paul the Apostle. Too often our parties seem to divide us into absolutely opposite religions. It is, above all, when we consider the suspicion and distrust, the rude recriminations, the unfair arguments, which separate different sections of the so-called religious world, — it is here that we begin to appreciate most fully the value of the Christian lesson furnished to us, at the close of the Book of Acts, by a Heathen example.

IX.

ONESIMUS.

"In time past to thee unprofitable, but now profitable to thee and to me." — PHILEM. 11.

THE Acts of the Apostles end by informing us that, on his arrival in Rome, St. Paul "dwelt two whole years in his own hired house, and received all that came in unto him, preaching the kingdom of God, and teaching those things which concern the Lord Jesus Christ, with all confidence, no man forbidding him." [1]

The cheerful tone of these words is remarkable. We cannot indeed help instinctively wishing that the narrative had been prolonged. We should have been glad to have read histories of the Apostle's conversations in Rome, and of the persons whom he met there, as copious and full as those which give so much varied interest to all the later chapters of this Book. But though the termination is abrupt, it is confident and sanguine. And this is the more worthy of note, if we consider carefully all the circumstances of the case. There were many things in St. Paul's condition at this time which might naturally have been disheartening and dispiriting. But

[1] Acts xxviii. 30, 31.

our last glance at the Great Apostle and his work, as afforded us by this Book, enables us to see them on the bright side. Either his own energetic and unyielding spirit communicated itself to his biographer, or St. Luke, cheering St. Paul by his companionship, wrote as he felt and as he enabled others to feel.

"Two whole years" in mature life is a large part of a laborious career. We must be careful, indeed, to lay stress on these two conditions — *mature life,* and a *laborious career.* In childhood two years would not be reckoned long, because, though such a period seems longer to the child than it does to older persons, it produces no evident results for the benefit of society at large. And, with an idle man, it is of very little moment whether he lives two years or twenty. In fact, the shorter period is perhaps to be preferred, because he has wasted less time, and his example has been less mischievous. But when life is in its mature strength, and when active usefulness is the habit of the life, then "two whole years" is a very long time.

No one will dispute that *St. Paul's* career was one of unceasing activity and toil; and at the moment of which we read here, there seemed to be a singular value in his life. There had been no cessation of his activity from the time of his being first sent out on his Missionary course with Barnabas from Antioch.[1] He was now, so far as we can ascertain, a little over

[1] Acts xiii. 3.

sixty years old. His health, too, was delicate; and it was evident that a few years would begin to make a great difference in his power of enduring fatigue and resisting the effects of sickness or privation. Thus there is a peculiar interest in what he did and what he suffered at this period of his life.

He was at this time a prisoner in Rome. And though he was far from having absolutely lost his freedom of speech and action, it is evident that such restraint must have involved much trial, with serious hindrances of the work to which he was devoted. His mode of employment in the midst of this combined bondage and liberty cannot fail to be peculiarly instructive; and though, as has been said, the narrative in the Acts ends abruptly, we are not without materials for obtaining large information on this subject. We shall however be better able to appreciate the full significance of the "two whole years," in Rome, if we revert for a moment to the circumstances which had preceded.

On looking back to the close of an earlier chapter, and to the last character but one that was under our consideration, we are reminded of another period of "two years."[1] St. Paul had been apprehended at Jerusalem, in the midst of a tumult, and sent to Cæsarea, where the Governor Felix resided: and here, too, he was a prisoner for this space of time, shut out from the active employments in which he always longed to be engaged. This condition of

[1] Acts xxiv. 27.

restraint had indeed its alleviations. Felix, as we recollect, did not treat him harshly. He gave orders to the centurion that he should allow St. Paul to have a considerable amount of liberty, "and forbid none of his acquaintance to minister or come unto him."[1] Still he was restricted to one place: and to a man of his temperament this must have been no slight trial. He saw how the companies of soldiers went and came along the great Roman roads which were connected with this city; but no such journeys were possible to him. He looked out over the sea, and saw the white sails of the ships, which kept up a busy traffic between this harbor and the far-off coasts; but he was not able to cross the water which separated him from Ephesus, or Corinth, or Rome. Whatever opportunities he might have of acting on the minds of others in conversation or by correspondence, this taking out of "two years" from the midst of his active career was a disappointment to which he would not easily submit, except by remembering that it was God's will.

At length the time came for his departure. "After two years" another governor succeeded. "Porcius Festus came into Felix's room; and Felix, willing to show the Jews a pleasure, left Paul bound." The events which followed under the governorship of Festus are told at length in the twenty-fifth and twenty-sixth chapters, though perhaps they occupied no very long period. The time was come when St.

[1] Acts xxiv. 23.

Paul was to cross this sea towards Rome, and, as we have seen, under the charge of one of these very soldiers. And now the voyage itself must be taken into account in connection with our present train of thought. It must be remembered that a ship is very often practically a prison, especially when it is crowded with people and the weather is stormy. Now we know that there were nearly three hundred people on board the vessel in which the Apostle Paul was wrecked.[1] The storm, too, had been so violent and prolonged, that great privations had been suffered by the whole crew.[2] There was also considerable detention at more places than one; and, on the whole, we cannot put the time spent between Cæsarea and Rome at less than half a year. Thus, with the two imprisonments, we have four years and a half to be taken out of a laborious career in mature life. When we wish to appreciate the exertions and the success of St. Paul, it behooves us to take into careful consideration all these sufferings and hindrances, and the probable effect of these things upon his health.

The Roman imprisonment, indeed, seems to have allowed even larger liberty and more alleviation than the former one at Cæsarea. Either the favorable report of Festus the Governor, who was much perplexed by the case, or the influence of Julius the Centurion, who evidently had a true affection and respect for St. Paul, or other circumstances of which we know nothing, caused him to have some of the

1 Acts xxvii. 37. 2 Acts xxvii. 18–21, 33, 34.

fullest privileges permitted to a prisoner. On his arrival in Rome, when delivered up to the Captain of the Guard, he was not forced into a dismal dungeon with a crowd of malefactors, but "suffered to dwell by himself with a soldier that kept him."[1] Some soldier was always his companion, with his own arm chained to St. Paul's arm. Such was the custom. He alludes to this when he addresses the Jews, whom, immediately on his arrival, he invited to visit him: "It is for the hope of Israel that I am bound with this chain."[2] Further on we are told that there was a large meeting of Jews "at his lodging." And then it seems that he changed his quarters, and, though still a prisoner, lived in a commodious house, of which, either by subscriptions in Rome or through the help of distant churches,[3] he was enabled to defray the cost; and the two last verses of the book are in the cheerful words which were quoted above.

Now, though a direct and detailed history is not given to us, we have both in the passage itself and elsewhere, very full materials for enabling us to appreciate the manner and results of St. Paul's employment during these "two whole years." We see, from the very wording of the passage, that large numbers of persons came to him. Besides this, the soldier who kept guard over him was frequently changed, and thus he must have made acquaintance with a considerable number of members of the army. But moreover, however much he was hindered from

1 Acts xxviii. 16. 2 Ver. 20. See Col. iv. 18. 3 See Phil. iv. 14.

travelling, he was not hindered from *writing.* We know what the letters were which he wrote at this time. They were the Epistles to the Philippians, to the Ephesians, to the Colossians, and to Philemon. Thus we have the most authentic resources, partly in the concluding words of the Book of Acts, partly in these four Epistles, for picturing to ourselves the employments and the companions of St. Paul during these "two whole years," and the opportunities which he possessed even then, and diligently used, for spreading the Gospel of Christ.

The mere fact of his writing these letters should be dwelt upon with attention. A time of imprisonment was favorable to this occupation. And what a powerful method of doing good was here within his reach! He could instruct distant churches, console them in their difficulties, rebuke their errors; and all that he thus set before them with such ends, being in writing, was their perpetual possession. They could refer to the words of their great teacher, consider them well, read them aloud, copy them down, study them in private, learn them by heart, place them side by side with their conduct, "for reproof, for correction, for instruction in righteousness."[1] But not only so: in writing thus he communicated with all future ages. As it has been truly and well said, "the restraint on St. Paul's liberty proved the means of opening to him a sphere of activity which has given him access to all nations, which makes him the con-

[1] 2 Tim. iii. 16.

temporary of every age." In writing to the Ephesians and Colossians concerning great doctrines; in writing to the Philippians concerning the example of Christ; in writing to Philemon concerning justice and mercy, he is speaking to us, if we will but listen to him, without let or hindrance, just as in Rome he personally "received all that came in unto him, preaching the kingdom of God, and teaching those things which concern the Lord Jesus Christ, no man forbidding him."

But we know, moreover, from these Epistles, much of his *personal intercourse*, and of the large effects which followed it. I say nothing at present of all those Christians who were in the Great City itself before St. Paul came there, and to whom messages had been conveyed by Phœbe in the Epistle to the Romans.[1] With most of these he doubtless made acquaintance. But I confine myself to the letters written at this period from Rome itself. Here, for instance, at the close of the letters to the Colossians and Philemon, are the names of Luke and Aristarchus, whom we know to have been his companions on the voyage from Cæsarea.[2] Here is Demas, up to the present time his "fellow-laborer," though afterwards he fell away, through that love of the world which is still the great enemy of the love of Christ.[3] Here is Mark, described now as a "fellow-worker

1 Rom. xvi. 1–16.
2 Col. iv. 10, 14; Philem. 24. See Acts xxvii. 2.
3 2 Tim. iv. 10.

unto the kingdom of God," and a "comfort" to the Apostle, though some years before he had been faithless, had "departed" from Paul, and "not gone with him to the work."[1] And, if we turn from these Epistles to that which was written, apparently somewhat later, to the Philippians, we seem to see that Luke has now left him, while Timotheus is with him.[2] Both are names very familiarly known in connection with the Church of Philippi.[3] Perhaps Luke had been sent to the Philippians. Paul certainly hopes to send Timothy soon. This large circle of friends at Rome is full of interest. It is a mark of the Apostle's great influence and power over the minds of others. And it is to be remembered that it is not merely friendship, to sustain and console, with which we are concerned here. But these names represent a large system of concurrent effort. He was the heart. He gave the pulsations from which strength and warmth and force came to them: so that they labored under him, and labored successfully. Thus we find him saying, in reference to those who were with him in Rome, "Many of the brethren in the Lord, waxing confident by my bonds, are much more bold to speak the word without fear."[4]

We may even pursue this train of thought further, so as to come to still more definite results, and from each of these four Epistles we may single out one friend and fellow-laborer of St. Paul, concerning

1 Acts xiii. 13; xv. 38.
2 Phil. i. 1; ii. 19.
3 Acts xvi. 12; xvii. 15; xviii. 5; xx. 6.
4 Phil. i. 14.

whom, at this period, we really have very full information. And in thus singling out individuals, and observing their personal relation with the Apostle, we see more of the inner working of his mind and heart — of the real principles on which he acted — than we could possibly see by the mere study of any general statements. We open the Epistle to the Colossians, and there we find, near the beginning, this said concerning *Epaphras*, that he is the Apostle's "dear fellow-servant," that he is "for them a faithful minister of Christ," and that he had also declared to St. Paul "their love in the Spirit;" but especially, near the end, we find this: "Epaphras, who is one of you, a servant of Christ, saluteth you, always laboring for you fervently in prayers, that ye may stand perfect and complete in all the will of God; for I bear him record that he hath a great zeal for you, and them that are in Laodicæa, and them in Hierapolis."[1] Now what a large amount of Christian love and coöperation comes to view from a careful examination of such a passage as this! What a consolidation and strengthening of scattered Christian communities it represents! And if Epaphras is the living link of connection between the Apostle and Colossæ with its neighboring cities, *Tychicus* holds the same relation towards the great community of Ephesus. The words concerning him are these. After asking the Ephesians to pray for him, and reminding them that he is "an ambassador in bonds,"

[1] Col. i. 7, 8; iv. 12, 13.

he says, "That ye may also know my affairs, and how I do, Tychicus, a beloved brother and faithful minister in the Lord, shall make known to you all things, whom I am sending to you for the same purpose, that ye might know our affairs, and that he might comfort your hearts."[1] Here is the same unceasing activity in a time of bondage; the same uncontrollable sympathy; the same features of personal intercourse; the same employment of a friend and companion for the strengthening of those who are far removed. But in illustration of all these points, perhaps the best examples are *Epaphroditus*, who is conspicuous in the Epistle to the Philippians, and *Onesimus*, whose fault and repentance gave occasion to the exquisite letter addressed to Philemon. Attention is first invited to the second of these two; and there is one special fact which invests his case with peculiar importance.

In the Roman Empire were a class of persons extremely numerous and universally diffused, of which we in England have happily no experience. In the city of Rome itself, probably half the population consisted of slaves: the greater part of the industrial labor, both in the metropolis and in the provinces, was in their hands; and very often they were highly educated. Thus, deplorable as their condition really was, they were very important members of society; and, of course, they were met at every turn. Now if Christianity is a beneficent system, coëxtensive in

[1] Eph. vi. 21, 22.

its remedial power with the evils which afflict humanity, one of its assigned functions must have been to ameliorate the condition of slaves, and to put an end to the system under which they suffered. The mode in which this has been gradually effected in the course of ages supplies material for one of the most instructive of all studies; and it receives a signal illustration from the short story of Onesimus.

The story is soon told. Onesimus was the slave of Philemon at Colossæ: he had robbed his master and run away; and, in the end, found his way to Rome. There, by some strange chance, as we should say, this runaway slave met with St. Paul, and under his teaching became a Christian. And now he was to be reconciled to his master. Such was the occasion of this most courteous and beautiful letter. The Apostle has to deal with a delicate subject; and he does this with consummate skill, and with the most delicate Christian tact. We might dwell upon this feature of it in detail. Or we might adduce this correspondence as a specimen of St. Paul's varied activity under circumstances when most men would have been discouraged, and tempted to relax their efforts. Or we might use it to illustrate another point. Not only, while a prisoner, is he unceasingly occupied in the diffusion of great doctrinal truths, but he can give his time and thought to a case of domestic discomfort, and to the interest of a fugitive thief. The point, however, selected for the present occasion, and that to which our thoughts have been tending, is this, that the short apostolic letter now before us elucidates the principle upon which a vast amount of human suffering has been alleviated, and a large proportion of the human race elevated from a degraded position to equal brotherhood with the rest.

Of the *character* of Onesimus, when converted to Christianity, we may just say this, that he became altogether a different man. "Begotten" to a new and spiritual life by St. Paul "in his bonds" at Rome, he is become the brother both of the Apostle himself and of the master who had been wronged. We find these new relationships briefly and strongly expressed in an Epistle which Onesimus himself conveyed; an Epistle which, with this subject before us, it is most instructive to compare with that to Philemon. In writing to the Colossians, St. Paul says he is sending Tychicus "with Onesimus, a faithful and beloved brother;" and then he adds, not without a most suggestive hint to the Christian residents at Colossæ: "who is *one of you*."[1] He who had been the slave of Philemon is now made the "brother" of the saints. He who had been a runaway thief is now worthy of the highest trust. To the Apostle himself in Rome he is so dear, that he speaks of him as "his very heart," as "his very self."[2] Onesimus shows, too, such capability of useful service, that he might take Philemon's own place in helping the Apostle, if only it were right to retain him without permission.[3] As regards Philemon, Onesimus is now, though still

[1] Col. iv. 9. [2] Philem. 12, 17. [3] Ver. 14.

bound to him by the tie of earthly service, a true spiritual brother. To him he is even more than he is to St. Paul. It is assumed that he is doubly dear to him, "both in the flesh and in the Lord."[1] The whole is summed up in the words that were quoted at the head of these remarks, words characterized even by a certain playfulness which is lost to the English reader. The Greek word "Onesimus" means "profitable;" and, knowing this, we detect a singular cheerfulness of confidence expressed in the saying that he who was "in time past unprofitable" to Philemon is now "profitable" to him as well as to St. Paul.

This change in the poor slave, and in the feelings that now surrounded him, is a sample of the influence which in time undermined the system of slavery. Let us see for a moment what this slave-system was in the Roman world. Bondmen at this period might be purchased, or might be taken as captives in war, or might be born of slave-parents in the household of their masters. To which of these sources the bondage of Onesimus is to be traced, we are not able to say. But this may be remarked, by the way, that Phrygia, in which the city of Colossæ was situated, was preëminently and proverbially a slave-producing region; so that even in this respect the case before us is a typical instance. Whatever the origin of the bondage in any particular case might have been, its condition was always most miserable. A slave had

[1] Ver. 16.

no legal personality. He was merely a living machine, and was viewed almost as belonging to the same class as the cattle on the farm or the furniture in the house. It is evidently natural that such a state of things should not only have marred the comfort of domestic life, but fostered the commission of crime and endangered the peace of society. The inevitable characteristics of slaves in the Roman Empire were theft and falsehood, and, when it was possible, conspiracy. Seneca, a contemporary of St. Paul in Rome, says: "Show me how many slaves there are, and I will show you how many enemies we have." Perhaps the saddest of all the circumstances connected with the system of ancient slavery was, that even the highest minds regarded it as a matter of course. They could hardly conceive of society as existing without it. We in England can hardly imagine the toleration of such an evil.

Now, one great office of Christianity has been the emancipating of the slave. But how? Not by vehemently telling him of his rights. Not by inflaming his indignation against his oppressors. This would have made Christ's kingdom "a kingdom of this world;"[1] would have sanctioned insurrection; would have excited under the Emperors a "Servile War;" like that which made havoc previously in the Republic; a war, too, which would have led to a reaction of still greater oppression and cruelty. The true solvent for this hard and bitter evil was *charity*, such

[1] John xviii. 36.

as was felt by the centurion of Capernaum,[1] such as was encouraged by St. Paul in Rome. The altering of the heart both of the master and the slave, the purifying of their motives, the softening of the affections of the master and the creating in him a spirit of justice, the raising of the slave up to a sense of duty, and the giving to him a hope which throws the accidents of our earthly condition into the shade,— this was the true Act of Emancipation. Thus the slave lost his vices; became loyal, truthful, honest; and the master, on the other hand, became considerate, kind, and just. Thus Slavery died, as it were, a natural death. The sentiments created by Christianity in due time pervaded the Christian commonwealth, and ultimately passed into usage and law.

We should observe, too, that this particular instance exemplifies what St. Paul says, in general terms, of the duties of masters and slaves. In that Epistle which has been referred to as intrusted to Onesimus, these duties are laid down.[2] In proportion as they were discharged in the right spirit, an approximation would take place between two naturally hostile sections of the community; and just as already "Jew and Greek" were made one, so, to quote again the same Epistle to the Colossians,[3] "bond and free" were made one. Onesimus stands, in fact, to one subject almost in the same relation in which Cornelius stands to the other. We cannot too carefully observe St. Paul's consistency with himself. He does

1 Luke vii. 2. 2 Col. iii. 22; iv. 1. 3 Col. iii. 11.

not urge Onesimus to insist on separation from his master, or even to demand his freedom. On the contrary, he sends him back. He may give a suggestion to Philemon, and may confidently express a hope that he will do "even more" than the Apostle says.[1] But the duty of Onesimus is clear. All is to be left to the operation of true Christian principle in the two men, according to the circumstances in which they are respectively placed. This is in strict harmony with what is enjoined in one of the Epistles to the Corinthians, that each man is willingly to abide in that calling where Christianity has found him. Nay, "is he called, being a slave?" He is "to use this servile condition all the more readily," that in it he may do all the more honor to Christ:[2] for such, whether he considers the context or the Greek, the careful student will perceive to be the true meaning of the passage. And Onesimus seems to have caught the true spirit of this great lesson. He has a full sense of the wrong done to Philemon, and is in no wise unwilling to return to Colossæ. It is instructive to see here how a great principle is involved in what seems at first sight a casual circumstance; and when we consider that by such methods as this Slavery has been gradually ceasing to exist, we feel that we have in the story of Onesimus a signal proof of the richness and expansiveness of Scripture.

1 Philem. 21.

2 1 Cor. vii. 21.

X.

EPAPHRODITUS.

"My brother, and companion in labor, and fellow-soldier, but your messenger, and he that ministered to my wants." — PHIL. ii. 25.

AUTHENTIC materials for obtaining a clear view of St. Paul's employments during his captivity in Rome, and for appreciating the use which he made there of his facilities for spreading the Gospel, are supplied by no Epistle so well as by that which was written to the Philippians; and of all those companions who surrounded him at that time, and became helpful, both in Rome itself and in regard to communication with distant churches, the best to select as a representative of the whole number is Epaphroditus, the bearer of this letter to Philippi.

As regards the Epistle, it is worth while, in the first place, to observe that, while it contains no slight or obscure indications of suffering and struggle, it gives the impression of great vigor and of success in conducting the apostolic work. St. Paul tells the Philippians that "he would have them understand that the things which had happened unto him had fallen out rather unto the furtherance of the Gospel." [1]

[1] Phil. i. 12.

His imprisonment, and the manner in which he had been able to bear his afflictions and to use his opportunities, had infused courage and zeal into the great majority of the Christian community in Rome. Some, indeed, he adds, were under the influence of inferior motives; but still, on the whole, there was marked progress.[1] And in the course of the Epistle there occurs the mention of two classes of persons with whom he was specially associated, and through whom the Gospel obtained a wide diffusion. These were the Imperial troops and the members of the Imperial household. What is called "the palace"[2] must really be understood as denoting the general body of soldiers in Rome, whether quartered on the Palatine or in the other parts of the city; and in the phrase "Cæsar's household"[3] all those are comprised, whether slaves, or freedmen, or officials of various ranks, who stood in some sort of personal relation to the Emperor. It is evident that in carefully attending to the two methods thus supplied for spreading the Truth of Christ, we are closely considering St. Paul's Companions.

As regards the Imperial household, from the Christian members of which salutations were sent with peculiar warmth to the Christians at Philippi, it is obvious, even at first sight, that any religious impression made here was likely to have great results. Officials of all kinds, touching every rank and condition of life, were in connection with that vast estab-

[1] Vers. 15–18. [2] Ver. 13. [3] Phil. iv. 22.

lishment. Moreover, that establishment was in the very centre of the civilized world, and had drawn into itself and assimilated very various national elements from all parts of the empire. Doubtless, too, Christianity had penetrated into this household before St. Paul himself arrived in Rome. This might almost be taken for granted from the very existence of the Epistle to the Romans, which had been sent from Corinth more than two years before the voyage from Cæsarea began.[1]

But we need not be limited to these general expressions. We are able to supply details from something more than mere conjecture, and to name with a high degree of probability some of the persons with whom St. Paul was brought in contact in the close neighborhood of the Court. In endeavoring to elucidate this point we naturally turn to that list of names, which is found in the last chapter of the Epistle to the Romans, and of which no use was made when Onesimus was our subject. Now it is a circumstance of very singular interest that some resting places of the dead, undoubtedly appertaining to members of Cæsar's household, and undoubtedly also belonging to the very time of St. Paul's sojourn in Rome, exhibit in connection with sepulchral ashes a large number of the very names which occur in this chapter. The writer of this paper can never forget the start of pleasure with which he saw the name of Tryphæna in one of these cells underground, and

[1] See Rom. xv. 25, 31; xvi. 1, 2.

then that of Tryphosa among the foliage in another part of the same vineyard. But many others of the identical names in the Epistle occur among these inscriptions. Some, indeed, such as Urban and Hermes, are common names, so as to cause no surprise. Others, such as Stachys and Patrobas, are comparatively rare, so as to arrest the attention more; while such a combination as that of Philologus and Julia deserves special observation, the former word appearing among these monuments, and the latter in itself indicating a connection with the Imperial family.[1] On the whole, though nothing can be absolutely proved, it is difficult not to believe that we have here in Modern Rome the ashes of some of those in the midst of whose companionship St. Paul preached the Gospel in Ancient Rome.

From the Imperial household to the Imperial troops the transition is easy and obvious. The word "palace" in our English Version itself supplies the natural link of connection. A large number of soldiers were quartered in the palace itself on the Palatine Hill; and among the most interesting remains of Imperial Rome are rude inscriptions scrawled by these rough soldiers on the plaster, at the very period when Christianity was young. Some have thought that St. Paul himself had his residence in one of these chambers. Others, perhaps with more

1 See the Bishop of Lincoln's *Tour in Italy*, vol. ii. p. 173, and especially Professor Lightfoot's *Commentary on the Philippians*, pp. 169–176.

probability, have imagined his dwelling to have been within the great Prætorian Camp, the position of which is still conspicuously marked by a great square inclosure on the north of the city. The most probable view of all is that the expression in the Epistle refers not to any exact place, but to the body of Prætorian guards, wherever they were stationed. The position of St. Paul's "hired house,"[1] may be left indeterminate, as of no moment in regard to our present subject. The point of importance is his continuous communication with the soldiers.

We know that the Apostle was freely allowed to see "all that came in unto him."[2] His conversations, then, were incessant; and they must have led to much subsequent discussion, resulting in the gradual diffusion of Christian faith and love. But a companion of one particular class, though the individuals were not the same, was with him night and day. A soldier was always by his side, with his own hand chained to the Apostle's hand. This circumstance furnished to him a remarkable opportunity for spreading the Gospel. The soldier who kept guard over him was frequently changed; and thus, in the course of the "two whole years," he must have made the intimate acquaintance of a considerable number of members of the army. As first one and then another relieved guard in this military duty, each of these rough men, in this intimate relation, would observe and wonder at the earnestness and zeal of this prisoner; would see

1 Acts xxviii. 30. 2 Acts xxviii. 31.

and hear him in his appeals to those "that came in unto him;" he would marvel at his intense earnestness in argument and in persuasion; at other times would see him studying such "books" as those which are mentioned in reference to a later imprisonment, and "especially the parchments,"[1] if we are to view them as denoting the Old Testament Scriptures; would watch that process of dictation, under which one part of the New Testament Scriptures came gradually into existence, and, above all, would watch him at his prayers, — those prayers, to which he alludes so constantly in the opening parts of his Epistles, and nowhere more emphatically than in those four Epistles which were written at this time in Rome.[2]

Each such soldier, when his duty was done, would go back to tell his comrades of this wonderful prisoner. Nothing like it had ever been known. It would be the talk of all the barracks. And, of course, it is obvious that the quarters of the soldiers were, more or less, in relation with all the city. Thus, by the exercise of a little careful thought, we begin to see the full meaning of the juxtaposition of the two sentences which St. Paul places together in the early part of what he writes to the Philippians: "I would that you should understand, brethren, that the things which happened unto me have fallen out rather unto the furtherance of the Gospel; so that my bonds in Christ are manifest to all the Prætorian troops and to

1 2 Tim. iv. 13.

2 See Eph. i. 16; Phil i. 4; Col. i. 3; Philem. 4.

all others elsewhere." It seems strange that a power of spreading the Gospel, which was denied to him in Jerusalem, the Holy City of Revealed Truth, should have been given to him in Rome, the profligate and cruel centre of the Heathen World; stranger still that this liberty of evangelization should have been exercised through the very soldiers who caused him to be perpetually a prisoner.

But again, the work done at the centre not only produced results in Rome, but affected a much wider circumference through the medium of the soldiers. These members of the Roman army were recruited from many barbarous nations on all the frontiers of the empire. They came from Britain, from Germany, from Africa, from the Danube, from the East. And, in turn, they were liable to be sent out to various and far distant places on foreign duty. An illustration of this is supplied by the case of the Centurion Julius, who has recently been under our direct consideration.[1] These troops in Rome were in organic connection with all the provinces. Thus the army itself became a kind of missionary organization; and there is little doubt that the ultimate establishment of Christianity in the empire owed a great deal to the spread of Christian thoughts and Christian feelings by these methods. Campaigns or civil wars took place frequently during this period; and in each great movement of Roman soldiers we can justly see a preparation for the receiving of the Gospel. Our own

[1] Acts xxvii. 1; xxviii. 16.

country, for instance, was just then in the process of being conquered; and as the victorious army pressed on afterwards, and established itself firmly in such places as London, Chester, and York, they would bring with them reminiscences of St. Paul; and thus the words spoken and the work done by this prisoner at Rome were among the causes that led to the founding of the early British Church. We have good reason to look back with thankfulness to what he was able to do in those "two years, no man forbidding him."[1]

Thus, through the medium of the soldiery, progress was made in the diffusion of the Gospel over the world, though the great Apostle of the Gentiles was stationary in his prison-house. But, in another and more emphatic sense, it is true, to use his own expression, that "the Word of God was not bound"[2] while he himself was in bondage.[3] "The care of all the churches" still pressed incessantly upon his active mind; and from this Imperial centre, whence troops, and governors, and judges were continually sent to all the provinces, St. Paul too dispatched his messengers with letters which have survived to our day, while military and political dispatches have been forgotten. We cannot too carefully bear in mind that the Companions of St. Paul stood to him in the place of postal arrangements. In the case of several of his Epistles, we can name the persons who conveyed them. For instance, Onesimus took, along

[1] Acts xxviii. 30, 31. [2] 2 Tim. ii. 9. [3] 2 Cor. xi. 28.

with the private communication to Philemon, those documents which are associated with the names of Ephesus and Colossæ; Phœbe was the bearer of the great letter from Corinth to Rome; and at an earlier period we find Titus engaged in the same way in connection with the Epistles to the Corinthians.

The correspondence of St. Paul with Philippi possesses an interest which is unique. No church was so dear to him; no church so thoroughly deserved, or so copiously received, his approval. In the midst of his thought of all the various Christian communities which he had founded, the remembrance of none was so pleasing to him as of this. He calls it "his joy and his crown." The circumstances under which the first converts were made at Philippi (and it must be regarded as highly probable that among these early converts was Epaphroditus) were of such a character as to leave an indelible impression on his memory. All his communications, too, with this church, since that first introduction of Christianity into Europe, had been satisfactory and cheering. The notices, indeed, of his two subsequent visits to Philippi, are but scantily given in the Acts.[1] But the Epistles reveal an intercourse, which indicates warm feeling and watchful thought towards the Apostle. This church, though not wealthy, as other churches were,[2] and though much tried by conflict and suffering, had supplied St. Paul's wants by generous contributions, both in Thessalonica, very soon after

[1] Acts xx. 3, 6. [2] See 2 Cor. viii. 2.

his departure from Philippi, and, at a later time, in Corinth.[1] Thus, by the recollection of his own sufferings, by the joy with which he beheld their victory over persecution, and by a sense of personal kindness shown to himself, St. Paul was specially bound in affection to the Philippians.

The occasion which brought Epaphroditus to Rome, and caused the writing of this Epistle, was a recurrence of their old generosity. They heard that he was in prison and in want. Thus, "now at the last their care of him flourished again."[2] The original expression, which is thus translated, is very beautiful. It reminds us of a tree, which, though it may have suffered in hard winters, and though it may have been severely handled by the axe, still lives and sends out fresh and vigorous shoots. Their wish, too, was not simply to send a certain sum of money safely to Rome, but to supply as much sympathy and comfort as possible to the Apostle in his time of difficulty and trial; and as the best representative of their own feelings, and the most likely person to make the gift acceptable, they chose Epaphroditus.

Now, to aid us in estimating aright the character of Epaphroditus, and his association with St. Paul in relation to the spread of the Gospel, we have a passage very copious in detailed information, while it is full of the tenderest feeling. St. Paul is now sending back Epaphroditus, of whom he gives this description: he is "my brother, and companion in

[1] 2 Cor. xi. 9. [2] Phil. iv. 10.

labor, and fellow-soldier, but your messenger, and he that ministered to my wants." Then he adds the reason why he is now sending him: "for he longed after you all, and was full of heaviness, because that ye had heard that he had been sick; for, indeed, he was sick nigh unto death; but God had mercy on him; and not on him only, but on me also, lest I should have sorrow upon sorrow: I am sending him, therefore, the more carefully, that, when ye see him again, ye may rejoice, and that I may be the less sorrowful." And further and most interesting information is supplied in the concluding words of the passage, where, after urging that Epaphroditus ought to be received "with all gladness," he gives this additional reason why he ought to be held in high honor, "because, for the work of Christ, he was nigh unto death, not regarding his life, to supply their lack of service towards him." By this last expression we are not to understand that there was any reluctance on the part of the Philippians in general to do service to St. Paul, but that Epaphroditus had done what those who were absent could not do, and what they would have done if they could. The words invite us to consider at length what Epaphroditus was to St. Paul, what he was to the Philippians, how he became a bond of closer union between the Apostle and this Macedonian Church, what his sufferings and feelings had been in time of sickness, and, further, what the actual cause of this sickness had been. Some very brief remarks on each of these five points are all that is possible here.

(1.) As to the estimate which St. Paul set on Epaphroditus, it is evident, in the first place, that sufficient time had elapsed since his arrival in Rome for the Apostle to know him well and to speak of him confidently. He was no mere casual acquaintance; and certainly St. Paul was not in the habit of using words at random. But we find him here accumulating the most honorable epithets in describing his friend. Epaphroditus is his "*brother*," his "*companion in labor*," his "*fellow-soldier*." The description is given in an ascending scale. Here are brought before us common sympathies in feeling, labors undertaken in common, and community in suffering and struggle. May we not also add — community in victory? It is clear that Epaphroditus has not been content with simply being the messenger of the Philippian Church, however prompt and faithful, and then stopping with the discharge of his errand. He has entered into St. Paul's case with much feeling; has thrown himself heartily into his work; has stood by his side in conflict. Other parts of the Epistle reveal to us that St. Paul had many opponents in Rome, and that some things involved to him a peculiar harassing of the mind. We cannot wonder, then, that he speaks warmly of Epaphroditus. We must mark, too, the personal gratitude expressed in the last phrase of the verse, — "he that ministered to my wants." It is very evident from this language that the Philippian "messenger" had not simply presented the money which he brought, but had contributed also his own thoughtful solicitude and encouragement. All this explains the deep emotion with which St. Paul asks that Epaphroditus, on his return to Philippi, may be "received in the Lord with all gladness," — and with which he thanks God for his mercy in having restored his friend to health, after a dangerous sickness, — lest, as he says, he himself should have had "sorrow upon sorrow."

(2.) Turning now, in the second place, to the relation of Epaphroditus with the Philippian Church, we see in him their willing and zealous *messenger*. He is the representative of their liberality. Evidently, too, he is no commonplace member of that community. His generous character corresponds with the errand on which he has been sent. And now he is about to be placed in a new relation to the Church in Philippi. Now *he is taking back to them this Epistle*, which is to fortify them and cheer them for whatever conflicts are still in store. Having "sown worldly things" in sending Epaphroditus to Italy, they are now, in his return, reaping "spiritual things"[1] for themselves and for all future ages. Among the journeys which come before our notice in the apostolic history, hardly any are more worthy of our attention and sympathy than those which Epaphroditus took from and to Philippi. And it is quite

[1] See 1 Cor. ix. 11.

worth our while to bear in mind that we are now, through the most modern arrangements for travelling, better able to realize the route than formerly. From Rome he would travel, as we should say, by Brindisi; and then, after crossing the Adriatic, would follow the great Roman road, which then intersected the mountainous country which we call Albania. Everything which gives freshness of outward circumstances to the ever-fresh lessons of the earliest Christian times has a value which ought not to be despised; and certainly Epaphroditus has a claim on our minute attention, as the worthy representative of a noble church.

(3.) We are thus brought to observe, thirdly, how Epaphroditus became a link of personal feeling between St. Paul and the Christians of Philippi, binding together more closely than ever the Apostle and his converts. The mere arrival of Epaphroditus in Rome must have made old memories more vivid, and kindled warm affections to a greater warmth. Questions innumerable would be asked concerning well-known friends of former days, concerning new accessions to the faith, concerning those who were gone to their rest. The gift, too, which Epaphroditus brought was made far more precious, and touched the Apostle's heart more tenderly, in being conveyed by such a man. Meanwhile, the anxiety which was felt in Philippi, through the news of their messenger's serious illness, became known to St. Paul. Thus an earnest wish was awakened in his mind to alleviate their sorrow. Great as was his own loss in seeing Epaphroditus depart, he was anxious that he should return at once, that when they "saw him again" they might "rejoice," and that, as he most generously adds, he himself might be "the less sorrowful." It would be difficult to find anywhere a more affecting interchange of affectionate feeling. It is a most forcible illustration of the truth that the "*whole body is joined together and compacted by that which every joint supplieth.*"[1] And in pursuing such reflections we see the advantage of studying the New Testament according to the biographical method. We thus learn how Christian feeling may be strengthened, and Christian hearts united, through individual exertion. This, too, is within the power of every one of us, if we use our opportunities aright, by putting ourselves in ready sympathy with those around us and with all whom we can help.

(4.) What has just been said suggests a fourth point, well worthy of distinct attention. Epaphroditus had been dangerously ill, causing much anxiety to St. Paul; and the news of this illness had reached the Philippians, causing distress to them. This feeling on their part was a sure indication that he was worthy of their love and esteem. But the point to which attention is here asked is this, that Epaphroditus was himself unsettled and unhinged, when he heard of this feeling among the Philippians. "He longed after them all, and was full of heaviness, *be-*

[1] Eph. iv. 16.

cause that they had heard that he had been sick." We like Epaphroditus none the less on this account. It brings him very near to ourselves. It is just what many of us have experienced, in times of nervous illness, when we know that friends are anxious, and when we think of home.

(5.) But one thing more must be noticed before we close. The origin of this serious and dangerous illness is made known to us. It was in the cause of the Gospel that this risk had been incurred. "*For the work of Christ* he was nigh unto death, not regarding his life." And the original Greek conveys the impression that there had been in Epaphroditus an imprudent zeal, a disregard of proper precautions, an overtaxing of his strength. The same causes have often since brought faithful ministers of the Gospel into jeopardy of their lives; and, though there is always something to regret in such imprudence, still enthusiasm and self-forgetfulness are admirable features of character, and such men ought to be "held in reputation."

As we leave the subject, there is a temptation to pause for a moment on a thought which is suggested by the sending forth from Rome such letters as those which were conveyed by Onesimus and Epaphroditus. Every eye is now turned with new and intense interest to what is taking place there.[1] May we not say

[1] This was written in the early part of the present year; and the substance of this paper was preached in a sermon at that time in the English Church at Nice.

that Paul is still *bound* in Rome? Nothing indeed can be more out of harmony with the spirit of these papers than harsh judgments on those who do not agree with the writer. Stern controversy has its place elsewhere, but not here. But even some Roman Catholics are now saying that one of the things most needed throughout the Roman Catholic communion, in seminaries for the education of the clergy, in parishes for the reading of the laity, is a thorough knowledge and intelligent appreciation of the doctrine and character of St. Paul. This, however, is, under present circumstances, quite impracticable. The course of history has been such that the Council of Trent, like Felix, "left Paul bound."[1] If only we could pour through the whole Roman Communion a flood of St. Paul's doctrine, well understood, vast benefits would follow to Christendom at large. But the fountain of this stream is frozen at Rome. While there every detached text which is supposed to reflect honor on St. Peter receives a colossal exaggeration, it is no breach of justice or charity to say that the whole continuous and elaborate teaching of St. Paul is thrown into the shade. Once, when he was literally a prisoner in Rome, his Epistles went forth freely from thence, to be the possession of the whole Christian people. Now this part of "the Word of God" is itself "bound" in Rome. Is not this contrast one of the most startling in history?

[1] Acts xxiv. 27.

XI.

AQUILA AND PRISCILLA.

"Aquila and Priscilla, with the church that is in their house." — 1 COR. xvi. 19.

NO religious book is less symmetrical and systematic than the Bible in its arrangement of doctrines and precepts; yet in no book is there so complete a code of faith and duty for all the varied circumstances of life. Broad and fearless in its statement of principles, it is also — if only there be that due exercise of judgment and of the individual conscience, which gives half its value to the observance of a religious rule — found to be really minute in its directions for conduct. In whatever condition we may be placed, light and guidance are always provided for us in the pages of Scripture. But these statements of principles, these directions for conduct, are not always obvious on the surface, and are often supplied where we should least expect to find them. Sometimes through the indirect teaching of an example, sometimes through words dropped incidentally, and by the way; sometimes by the relation of casual circumstances, which unexpectedly reveal great truths; it is thus, in regard to very important matters, that we learn to "understand what the will of the Lord is." [1] Hence the full benefit of the Scriptures is not to be got except by patient search and close comparison. The careless reader misses much. The diligent and well-equipped student is often surprised when he finds how parts of the Bible, which seemed intended for no such purpose, are "profitable for doctrine, for reproof, for correction, for instruction in righteousness." [2] In this, as in all things, it is discovered in the end that "Wisdom is justified of her children." [3]

The truth of these general remarks has already received some elucidation through two of the present series of slight biographies. In the case of Onesimus we have been brought face to face with the great problem of Slavery, and we have there seen how Christianity deals with it; not by violence, not by fomenting insurrection and war, but by gentleness, by forbearance, by mutual trust, by the sense of justice in every relation of life; and we have seen how this instance encourages us to believe that these methods must in the end have their sure result in the abolition of Slavery. Yet who would have expected our instruction regarding so great a question to have been found in so casual and incidental a part of the Bible as the Epistle to Philemon? [4] Again, it is in the same indirect manner that we receive one of our most instructive lessons regarding the value and the duty of Courtesy. Julius, the Heathen Centurion, reminds us that this commonplace, but often neglected virtue,

[1] Eph. v. 17.
[2] 2 Tim. iii. 16.
[3] Matt. xi. 19.
[4] Philem. 16, 21.

is not only the best policy, but also an imperative rule of Christian life.[1] And — to turn to a third instance — when we close this series, in the last paper, with a notice of Timotheus, we shall see how a subject which we feel to be a vital matter, and which is just now under the most serious discussion in all parts of our country, is spread before us only after close examination of a context, which at first sight appears intended for another purpose. The necessity of a religious education for our children might be expected to be one of the primary duties urged upon us in a revelation from heaven; yet nowhere in the New Testament do we find this laid down in any formal and precise manner. The case, however, is presented to us, in its whole breadth and its happy results, and with far greater force and encouragement than any mere enactment could have supplied, in what we are told of the early childhood of Timotheus, and of those holy influences which passed into his character and prepared him for his coming duties.[2]

Another topic is now before us. The true unit of social life in the Church is found in the life of those who are joined together in marriage. Nothing can be of more vital consequence than the manner in which this subject is presented to us in Scripture. We should of course expect the duties of husband and wife to be laid before us there in very clear and copious language. And this we do find. Two Apos-

1 Acts xxvii. 3, 31, 43.

2 2 Tim. i. 5; iii. 14, 15.

tles devote a definite and a very emphatic part of their writings to this topic. What St. Peter says in his First Epistle,[1] added to what we read in St. Paul's Epistles to the Ephesians and Colossians,[2] supplies a most complete and most sacred code for married life. And yet there are some things to be learned in regard to this state in its relation to the well-being of the Church, which no mere catalogue of duties, however authoritative and earnest, could ever have taught; and it is remarkable that in connection with the history of each of these Apostles there is the notice of a married couple, — such as in one case to supply a most awful warning, in the other a most cheering and most useful example.

In connection with the life of St. Peter — "himself a married man," as we are pointedly reminded in our Service for Holy Matrimony,[3] — we have Ananias and Sapphira teaching, and teaching for our solemn admonition, by example. In accounts of great crimes nothing shocks us so much as conspiracy and deliberate compact in evil. To be alone in the commission of willful sin is dreadful; but a far deeper guilt is incurred when there has been a calm mutual understanding preparatory to the perpetration of the wrong. And when those who are united together in the most sacred of bonds have joined together in the commission of crime, then, indeed, we have an illustration of the true proverb, that the worst thing in the world

[1] 1 Peter iii. 1-7. [2] Eph. v. 22-33; Col. iii. 18, 19.
[3] See Matt. viii. 14; 1 Cor. ix. 5.

is the corruption of the best. The history of Ananias and Sapphira must stand out in awful prominence, to warn us that a curse instead of a blessing may enter within the circle which was intended to be the holiest and happiest on earth, and that the husband and the wife, instead of strengthening one another in doing and suffering God's will, may make one another strong and fearless in sin and shame.

St. Paul was himself unmarried, and held strongly to the view that it was an advantage to his work that he should so remain.[1] And this circumstance tends to throw out into stronger relief the married life of Aquila and Priscilla, which is to be the subject of our present thoughts. We are to view them, not in their relation to one another, but as his Companions, and as through that Companionship doing good service to the Church. If, with this thought in our minds, we take in succession the five passages where this wedded pair is mentioned, we shall not find it difficult to deduce from them useful instruction, quite as applicable to our own times as to those of the Apostles.

(1.) The meeting of St. Paul with Aquila and Priscilla is, in the first place, an illustration of *the providential opportunities of life.* He had recently, when travelling on his Second Missionary Journey, "departed from Athens and come to Corinth." Just then it happened that the Emperor "Claudius had commanded all Jews to depart from Rome." We

[1] 1 Cor. vii. 7, 8, 40; ix. 5. See Matt. xix. 12.

need not enter here into any speculation concerning the reason for this harsh edict. Among these Jews, "lately come from Italy," was one of Pontus, "named Aquila, with his wife Priscilla." In them the Apostle found congenial companions: "and because he was of the same craft, he abode with them and wrought; for by their occupation they were tent-makers."[1] Now who would have expected such companionship to have been provided at this time and place? Pontus — known to us otherwise through St. Peter's first Epistle, but at a later period, as the home of certain Christians[2] — was very remote alike from Jerusalem and from Rome. Aquila and Priscilla had been brought to Rome through some of the exigencies of trade. Thence, in consequence of the Emperor's edict, they had moved eastward, possibly intending to return to Pontus, and meanwhile exercising their craft in the great mercantile city of Corinth, which lay on the route. At that moment St. Paul was moving southwards to the same place. The synagogue would of course be a bond of union between himself and these strangers. But another and very close bond was found in the trade in which both he and they had been trained. It was a wise Jewish maxim that every man, however wealthy might be the family to which he belonged, ought to learn a trade. Here we see the unexpected blessing which came to Saul of Tarsus through having learnt the business of tent-making; for it secured to him, at

1 Acts xviii. 1–3. 2 1 Pet. i. 1.

this critical time, a close friendship, with all its opportunities for furthering religious work, and all its cheerful solace to himself. Such a meeting was very remarkable. Yet it occurred quite, as we say, in the natural order of events. And God provides for us, in the natural order of events, meetings quite as remarkable. One of our greatest responsibilities consists in our using aright such providential opportunities.

Let it now be remarked that the friendship thus formed at Corinth is an illustration of the *right use* of providential opportunities. We need not give any attention here to the question whether Aquila and Priscilla had been converted to Christianity before they met St. Paul. That point does not affect what is here so strongly urged. In due time, if not from the first, these friends became hearty Christians together, helping each other to do God's work more effectually than they could have done separately. We shall see, as we pursue the history, how very far this union of kindred spirits was a mere friendship, valued for its own sake and ending in itself.

Still it is quite to our purpose to observe that this companionship provided *solace for St. Paul* at a time when it was much needed. He had been "left at Athens" alone; and the manner in which this circumstance is mentioned by himself[1] seems evidently to imply that the time which he spent in that frivolous city, as well as the early part of his visit to Corinth,

[1] 1 Thess. iii. 1.

was a time of depression and discouragement. This inference, too, is confirmed by the strong language used in the Acts [1] of the new impulse which his spirit received when Timotheus and Silas, on coming from Macedonia, rejoined him. To this we must add what he himself says of the "fear and trembling" and the sense of "weakness" which took possession of him during his early days at Corinth [2] — a statement which again is confirmed by a vision recorded in St. Luke's narrative, — where the Lord is described as saying to him by night, "Be not afraid, but speak, and hold not thy peace; for I am with thee, and no man shall set on thee to hurt thee; for I have much people in this city." [3] It is evident, too, that the utter profligacy of Corinth must have been a perpetual distress to St. Paul, and that all the associations of the place must have been alien from his sympathies. Putting all these things together, we learn to appreciate the value of the home he unexpectedly found here at this time. Though sternly separated from any domestic life of his own, Divine Providence had prepared for him, not only "an open door" for his missionary work, but the soothing refreshment of domestic society. The married life of Aquila and Priscilla was made helpful to him without placing him under any restraint. This is a point to which we are invited to give special attention in this part of St. Paul's life. Devoted missionary though he was, his

[1] Acts xvii. 15; xviii. 5. [2] 1 Cor. ii. 3.
[3] Acts xviii. 9, 10.

disposition was removed as far as possible from moroseness. The society of this godly and intelligent matron is to be taken into account among the circumstances which strengthened and cheered him in his work; and those who have the happiness of ruling over settled Christian homes may learn here that one of the highest forms of hospitality is to provide religious sympathy and cheerful intercourse for those who might otherwise be depressed in their solitary round of service.

(2.) We now follow St. Paul, and Aquila and Priscilla along with him, from Corinth to Ephesus. [1] Possibly his movements in some degree determined theirs. Or, on the contrary, the exigencies of business may have taken them across the Ægean, and thus afforded to him a convenient opportunity for accomplishing part of his return-journey. He had determined to spend an approaching festival at Jerusalem. Meanwhile they remained at Ephesus, with the promise and expectation of the Apostle's return. [2] It cannot be doubted that one definite purpose in these arrangements was that they should continue the work which, even in this short stay at Ephesus, had been begun by St. Paul, and should prepare the way for future and more systematic work on his return. And an occasion speedily presented itself for doing signal service in this way. Doubtless the case of *Apollos* was only one of many cases in which their help was exerted; but it is singled out as an instructive specimen for our attention.

[1] Acts xviii. 18. [2] Acts xviii. 21.

It is needless to repeat here what was said in an earlier paper concerning Apollos. We then considered some part of what may be learnt on *his* side of this meeting with Aquila and Priscilla. His willingness to learn, and to learn from a woman, notwithstanding his eager zeal and the admiration which his high talents excited, was noted as an example worthy and yet difficult of imitation. *Now* it is our part to observe *their* side, and especially *hers*. Their zeal for Christ made them quick-sighted in discovering the capabilities of Apollos; and they at once devoted themselves to the task of equipping him more completely for his high service. Their sound judgment and mature character fitted them for this task; and they were enabled to communicate to him that full Christian teaching which they themselves had received from St. Paul. In the office which this wedded pair performed for Apollos and the Church, a great part must obviously be assigned to the ready sympathy and tact of Priscilla. From the very fact that her name is always mentioned with her husband's we might infer that she possessed high qualities, if not that her character was the more energetic of the two; and it is worthy of notice, in connection with this view, that in three of the five places where the names occur, Priscilla, according to the true reading of the text, is mentioned before Aquila.[1] And at least we may trace in this occurrence at Ephesus a signal illustration of the truth that in Christ's active service, as

[1] Acts xviii. 26 ; Rom. xvi. 3 ; 2 Tim. iv. 19.

well as in the blessings of his salvation, there is "neither male nor female,"[1] and that women as well as men have their responsible and efficient part to play in advancing God's kingdom.

Nor ought we to fail in noticing how the warm-hearted and painstaking efforts of Aquila and Priscilla at Ephesus reacted on the place where they had originally made acquaintance with St. Paul. When Apollos was "disposed to pass into Achaia,"[2] they encouraged him to do this; letters of commendation were supplied to him; and when he came to Corinth, he "helped them much which had believed through grace." St. Paul had instructed Aquila and Priscilla at Corinth; they instruct Apollos at Ephesus; and he then passes on to Corinth to "water" where the Apostle had "planted."[3] So true it is that the streams of God's providence move hither and thither, and often turn back to the place from which they originarly moved.

(3.) Whilst Aquila and Priscilla remain at Ephesus, St. Paul now arrives, according to his promise, and rejoins them. We discover this by the salutation from these friends transmitted by him in the First Epistle to the Corinthians, which was written in Ephesus; and here it is that we first encounter that beautiful expression,[4] — "*the church that is in their house.*" Again we are invited, as we follow the notices of this godly pair, to look at Christianity on

[1] Gal. iii. 28. [2] Acts xviii. 27. [3] 1 Cor. iii. 6.
[4] 1 Cor. xvi. 19. See Rom. xvi. 5; Col. iv. 15; Philem. 2.

PAUL AT EPHESUS.

its domestic side. No side of our religion is more important; and first let a word be said, in passing, on the subject of Family Prayer.

Amid much that is cause for regret in the religion of modern England, we trace one bright feature of it in the institution of Domestic Worship. Other ages of the Church, and other countries of Christendom, have not been equally marked by this excellent practice; and it is earnestly to be hoped that no relaxation of the habit will take place amongst us. The family is thus recognized as the real unit of Church life; a sacred fire is kept burning upon the domestic hearth; and members of the same household are taught to consider themselves joined together by a higher bond than that which belongs to mere nature.

But if we turn back from our own times to those in which Aquila and Priscilla lived, we see a different, if not a higher, significance in the phrase which is before us. Those were times of peril and rebuke. We see here hospitality on what may truly be called its heroic side. The "house" of Aquila and Priscilla was devoted to something very different from that mere domestic comfort, the overvaluing of which is one of the weak points of modern English society. Their home was the acknowledged place of meeting to the disciples of Christ, for instruction, for worship, and for mutual help; and this involved ridicule, and might at any time involve violence, and even death. We see still the same characteristic in this household as before, when it provided a home for St. Paul at

Corinth. Still the husband and the wife are mentioned side by side, as coöperating, and, indeed, as being *one*, in the same good work. But now the home is provided for others besides St. Paul. The followers of Christ were all welcome there. It might truly be said that, in acting thus, they gave a home to Christ Himself. In his persecuted followers "He was a stranger, and they took Him in;" and the promised blessing was theirs; inasmuch as they did it "to one of these his brethren, they did it unto Him."[1]

(4.) No very long interval elapsed between the writing of the First Epistle to the Corinthians from Ephesus, and the writing of the Epistle to the Romans. But in this interval, for reasons which we are not able to supply, Aquila and Priscilla had returned to Rome, whence originally they had been exiled by the Emperor. They naturally have the first place in the long list of Christians resident in Rome, to whom the Apostle sends salutations;[2] and their characteristics remain the same. Once more their hospitality is prominent. "*The church in their house*" is named here again. As in Corinth, as in Ephesus, so in the great metropolis of the empire, they have the high distinction of making their home a shelter for those who professed the name of Christ, and a means for consolidating and extending his Church. They share, indeed, this distinction with others, — with Nymphas, for instance, at Colossæ;[3] and the case of

[1] Matt. xxv. 35, 40. [2] Rom. xvi. 3–5. [3] Col. iv. 15.

Philemon there is still more closely similar, because in the mention of Appia[1] we can hardly fail to recognize the name of his wife. But Aquila and Priscilla must always be the typical examples of domestic Christianity and of hospitality in its highest form.

The very occurrence of their names here, in this part of the Epistle to the Romans, gives a wide range to their example, and seems to connect them with the whole world. But the context makes some additions, which tend further to raise them to a position of high eminence. They are said by the Apostle not only to have been "his helpers in Christ Jesus" — which, indeed, the passages already quoted show that they were, — but to have "*laid down their own necks for his sake.*" This points to some heroic facing of danger on his behalf. It is not of importance here to determine where this took place. The probability is that it was at Ephesus, where, according to the Acts of the Apostles,[2] circumstances of great peril occurred to the Apostle at the time when Aquila and Priscilla were with him in that city. The personal gratitude of the Apostle breaks out warmly in this passage, "To whom not only I give thanks, but *all the churches of the Gentiles.*"

Here it is well worth while to refer to the apt, and yet incidental, correspondence of this expression with the history. Even at Corinth, where we first see these disciples with St. Paul, there had been great opposition on the part of the Jews. Aquila and

1 Philem. 2.

2 Acts xix. 21; xx. 1.

Priscilla adhered to St. Paul; hence they would be viewed as deserters from the Jewish cause, and would share his persecution. They were "*Jews taking part with Gentiles*, — and in that which was the great controversy of the day, the admission of the Gentiles to a parity of religious situation with Jews."[1] The accord, however, of the history and the Epistles, though full of interest and highly important, is not our present subject. It is the *character* of Aquila and Priscilla, in *companionship* with St. Paul, which now occupies our attention. And may we not say that we, too, as "Gentiles," have reason to give them "thanks," both for their aid in the first spread of the Gospel, and for the example which they have left to our homes?

(5.) Our limit of space being reached, no other use shall be made of the one remaining allusion to these friends of St. Paul, in his latest Epistle,[2] except to remark that the friendship, tried and strengthened through such variety of experience, *continued to the end.* Shortly before his martyrdom, he sends to them a loving salutation — the only salutation in this affecting letter, — the sharers of it with Aquila and Priscilla being "the household of Onesiphorus;" so that the domestic aspect of Christian life is doubly made conspicuous and charming at the very close of the Apostle's career.

There is another side of the biography of Aquila and Priscilla which might have been employed for

[1] Paley's *Horæ*, Paulinæ, ii. 2. [2] 2 Tim. iv. 19.

a very instructive lesson. They were examples of the combination of active Christianity with *industrial life ;* and no combination is of greater importance in our own times. But it seemed best to follow one principal train of thought in this short paper. Wedded life in combination with active Christianity is the very central point of the safety and happiness of society. Domestic duties within the household are of course the most important of all. But the married state has opportunities for exerting powerful influence far beyond its direct and immediate responsibilities. This has been taken as our present subject; and the manner in which it is exhibited to us in these incidental passages of the New Testament illustrates well what was said at the outset concerning the completeness of the Bible in regard to all moral teaching, though without careful and minute study that completeness cannot be fully known.

XII.

TIMOTHEUS.

"As a son with the father, he hath served with me in the Gospel."
PHIL. ii. 22.

IN our little gallery of "The Companions of St. Paul," the last panel must be filled with a slight sketch of Timotheus. For many reasons it is evident that he is the fittest to conclude the series. This disciple was associated with the Apostle through a longer range of time than any other of whom we have record. Joining him at an early period of his missionary enterprise, he remained in close communication with him till near the very time of his martyrdom. As a personal witness, he "had fully known" the sufferings of the Apostle; in fact — and this is the literal meaning of the Greek word in the passage,[1] — he had followed these sufferings step by step. He had been actively employed by his master, on responsible errands, in various places, through many years. In Epistles written on several occasions at wide intervals, from Corinth, from Ephesus, from Rome,[2] his name is coupled with St. Paul's so closely

[1] 2 Tim. iii. 10, 11.
[2] 1 Thess. i. 1; 2 Thess. i. 1. Compare 2 Cor. i. 1; also, Phil. i. 1; Col. i. 1; Philem. 1.

in the opening sentence, that he seems almost identified rather than associated with him. To Timotheus alone are two extant letters personally addressed; and letters, too, marked with so peculiar a tenderness of feeling, and so minute a mention of details, as to single him out very strongly and definitely as the friend for whom St. Paul's personal preference was the greatest. Whatever of intimacy, confidence, and sympathy is implied in the word "companionship," is in this case the most intense.

Our best course is to follow the life of Timotheus chronologically, making such reflections from point to point as naturally suggest themselves. Thus, too, we shall see what he was successively in relation to the other Companions of St. Paul, we shall join together some links which as yet are unfastened, and shall obtain a view over this whole cycle of apostolic friends. The Epistles enable us to begin this survey from an earlier point than any which is presented to us in the Acts of the Apostles, and show us something of the training of Timotheus even in his childhood, and therefore something of his preparation for that subsquent usefulness which marked his career when it became connected with that of the Apostle of the Gentiles.

The first actual mention of Timotheus in St. Luke's narrative is in the sixteenth chapter of the Acts, where he is described as the son of a Jewess who had become a Christian.[1] This prominent men-

[1] Acts xvi. 1.

tion of *his mother* is somewhat remarkable; and from another source we learn her actual name, and something, too, of her character. St. Paul, in his latest letter, when writing of the "unfeigned faith" that was in Timotheus, adds that such faith had "dwelt first in his grandmother Lois, and his mother Eunice;"[1] and in another part of the same document he charges him "to continue in the things which he had learned, knowing of whom he had learned them; and that from a child he had known the Holy Scriptures."[2] Thus we see that on the woman's side of this family there had been, for two generations at least, the inestimable blessing of hereditary piety.

It is not a little remarkable that a character which is among the most faultless and charming in the Bible, should be the character of that one person whose domestic relations and early training are thus described. And this circumstance is the more observable, if we can trace, as we can almost certainly, something of a feminine softness in Timotheus, as though his mother's gentle influence had passed into his mind and disposition. The *method*, too, of his early training is very important for us to notice. It was the method of *Biblical instruction*. "From a child he knew the Holy Scriptures." Those Scriptures, of course, in his case were the Old Testament. We are richer than the Jews by reason of possessing the New Testament in addition. This does not diminish,

[1] 2 Tim. i. 5. [2] 2 Tim. iii. 14, 15.

but rather infinitely increases, the weight we should attach to the Bible as an instrument of instruction. But again, not only the method, but the *spiritual principle*, which was at work in this process, should be noticed. Even in the Acts of the Apostles the *faith* of Eunice is made prominent; and here we see that it was the ruling power of life both in her case and in that of Lois. This passage of Holy Writ is full of admonition to Christian households as to the training of the young, and full of encouragement as to the happy results which may be expected from such training.

In tracing now this biography onward, we are able still to insert another stage of it before we reach the point where the first mention of Timotheus occurs in the Acts. St. Paul had been at Lystra previously to the time when this young disciple actually joined him there as his travelling companion.[1] Moreover, the Apostle speaks of him as "his own son in the faith,"[2] which seems to imply beyond a doubt that he himself was the instrument of his conversion. On the occasion, too, of this second visit Eunice is described as already a believer. All these circumstances point to the conclusion that Timotheus was converted on the occasion of the first visit. And this derives a strong confirmation from a passage, already noticed, in the Second Epistle to Timothy.[3] There it is said that he had fully known and closely followed "the persecutions and afflictions" which came to St. Paul

1 Acts xiv. 6. 2 1 Tim. i. 2. 3 2 Tim. iii. 11.

"at Antioch, at Iconium, at Lystra." Now, these sufferings occurred to St. Paul on the first visit; and the order in which the places are mentioned is the exact geographical order in which he was exposed to these trials. And this again leads to another thought. Such sufferings and ill-treatment incurred by one who is beloved and respected, make a deep impression upon a young mind; and we see in this earliest acquaintance of St. Paul and Timotheus the foundations deeply laid of a warm attachment and allegiance of the latter to the former, as well as an admirable preparation for arduous work and strong endurance. Nor must we forget that the circumstances thus related would bring Timotheus into personal acquaintance with St. Paul's earliest missionary companions; and we cannot well doubt that at this time he became familiar with the noble countenance of him whom the rude Lycaonians instinctively "called Jupiter," as well as with the voice of him whom they named "Mercurius, because he was the chief speaker."[1]

Barnabas ceased to be St. Paul's missionary companion, and Silas was taken in his place.[2] We have now passed from the First Missionary Journey to the Second, and are brought to the association of Timotheus with St. Paul in the actual work of evangelization. This point in the apostolic history is carefully marked by St. Luke; and it is full of instruction for us as to the duty of requiring in those who

[1] Acts xiv. 12. [2] Acts xv. 36–41.

are to be placed in high ministerial offices the qualification of ascertained fitness. We should also set the passage side by side with sentences in each of the two Epistles to Timotheus. Just as St. Paul urged the memory of this disciple's mother and grandmother to stimulate him to consistency and progress in piety, so he urges him to "stir up the gift of God,"[1] which manifestly had been bestowed upon him at the time of the "laying on of hands" by the Apostles and the general body of the presbyters. Evidence was fully supplied as to his personal character at this time. "He was well reported of by all the brethren that were at Lystra and Iconium." A further reason also for the choice is to be discovered in the words which follow: "Him would Paul have to go forth with him." It is not obscurely intimated here that there was something in Timotheus which won the Apostle's *personal affection*. He seems to have perceived from the very first — to quote the phrase which he used long afterwards of this friend — that he was "like-minded" with himself;[2] and great must have been his joy to have found such a companion in the very neighborhood which, a few years before, had been the scene of so much injustice and suffering, at a time, too, when he had been mourning over the defection of Mark.[3] And a further point of fitness for this moment of missionary work remains to be noted. It was a crisis in the history of the Church,

[1] 1 Tim. iv. 14; 2 Tim. i. 6. [2] Phil. ii. 20.
[3] Acts xiii. 13; xv. 38.

in regard to the relation between Judaism and Christianity. More need not be said in order to show that in the choice of a fellow-worker for Paul's future labors there was peculiar wisdom in selecting one whose mother was a Jewess, while "his father was a Greek."

The devotion of Timotheus, and the devotion of his mother also, were shown by his willingness to leave her for Christ's service; and the blessing was theirs which the Lord Himself promised to such "forsaking" of home "for his name's sake."[1] We now pass to the active employment of Timotheus in missionary work, on this Second Apostolic Journey, in conjunction with St. Paul and his other companions. One such companion has already been named; and presently, at the moment of passing over into Europe, he became associated with St. Luke also.[2] From this point he took part in the whole Macedonian round, and became one of the founders of the great churches of Philippi and Thessalonica. His name, indeed, is not mentioned by St. Luke in connection with either place. But we have the Apostle's weighty words in testimony of his faithful service at the former city: "*Ye know the proof of him*, that as a son with his father, he served with me in the Gospel."[3] That he was not imprisoned there with Paul and Silas, is easily accounted for by his comparative youth and subordination. There might, indeed, be some timidity in his conduct; but we trace his

[1] Matt. xix. 29. [2] Acts xvi. 10–13. [3] Phil. ii. 22.

subordination by the order of the three names in the Epistles written soon afterwards to Thessalonica;[1] and it should be remarked, by the way, that these Epistles imply a familiar knowledge of him in that city also. Passing on from Thessalonica to Berœa, we find him brought into contact with earnest discussions on the meaning of those Scriptures,[2] with which he had been made so well acquainted in his childhood at home; and here his name reappears in the text of the narrative. It is stated that he and Silas were left behind in Macedonia with instructions to rejoin the Apostle as soon as their errand should be discharged; and they did rejoin him when he was established in Corinth.[3]

It was arranged in the course of God's providence that St. Paul should have no companion with him in Athens; and the fact that he was "alone"[4] in that city, enhances the force of the unique impression we receive from that most remarkable passage of his life. But what we read of the effect produced upon his mind and work, when Timotheus, with Silas, rejoined him, tends to show us how much his happiness was increased by the presence of his friends, and what a reserve of true religious force resided for him in the mere fact of companionship. Some are too ready to throw upon others the work which they ought to do themselves; but he increased in zeal and activity when he could obtain others to help him. The literal

1 1 Thess. i. 1; 2 Thess. i. 1.
2 Acts xvii. 11.
3 Acts xvii. 14, 15; xviii. 5.
4 1 Thess. iii. 1.

meaning of the passage is, that on their coming he was "engrossed" or "absorbed" in "the Word."[1] The Epistles to Thessalonica, the writing of which followed close upon the arrival of Timotheus, show the high estimate which St. Paul had formed of him. In allusion to the mission with which he had been recently charged, he describes him as "*his brother*," as "*the minister of God*," and as "*his fellow-laborer in the Gospel of Christ*." Nor ought we to fail to notice the confidence implied in the mission itself. Serious troubles had occurred in Thessalonica; and this young disciple was sent to "establish" them and to "comfort them concerning their faith," so that they "should not be moved by these afflictions."[2] Even this slight notice of what took place during the Apostle's journey in Macedonia and Achaia, affords a testimony to many excellent and remarkable qualities in one so young, and so lately introduced into the work of missionary life. It is evident also that the journey afforded opportunities for gaining invaluable experience.

We have no means of supplying any information concerning Timotheus in the interval between the residence at Corinth, and the time when the Third Missionary Journey was well begun. He and Silas were, as we have seen, together with the Apostle at Corinth. There is every reason to believe that they travelled with him thence, touching at Ephesus on the way, to "the feast in Jerusalem."[3] Possibly

[1] Acts xviii 5. [2] 1 Thess. iii. 2, 3. [3] Acts xviii. 21.

Silas remained in Jerusalem. At all events, we do not trace him in company with St. Paul on the subsequent journey. But Timotheus is with him still. And when the Apostle is at Ephesus, we find him going over once more, in compliance with his desire, on an errand into Macedonia. Here his name is associated with that of Erastus, as formerly with that of Silas. "Paul purposed in the spirit, when he had passed through Macedonia and Achaia, to go to Jerusalem: so he sent into Macedonia two of them that ministered to him, Timotheus and Erastus."[1] In this we see the same obedience and alacrity on the part of Timotheus; the same confidence on the part of St. Paul. The mode of expression shows that they were intended to prepare his way. If Timotheus was to occupy himself with the details of the collection which St. Paul was at this time busily promoting, even that implied a character well known to be honorable, discreet, and trustworthy. But if he was commissioned to endeavor to assuage the party spirit and to correct the abuses at Corinth, qualities were implied of a yet higher and rarer kind. That he was directed to proceed to Corinth we have good proof; and the terms in which he is spoken of in the first Epistle to that place, written soon after his departure, deserve attention. St. Paul says in one passage: "I have sent unto you Timotheus, who is *my beloved son*, and *faithful in the Lord*, who shall bring you into remembrance of my ways which be in Christ, *as I teach everywhere in every church.*"[2] Nothing can

1 Acts xix. 21, 22. 2 1 Cor. iv. 17.

be more expressive of deep affection and confidential trust; and it may be added by the way, that if Timotheus knew so well what the Apostle taught "everywhere in every church," it seems natural to infer that he had been with him in many places, where no mention occurs of his name. We are not surprised to read what he says in another part of the same letter, "If Timotheus come, see that he may be with you without fear, for he worketh the work of the Lord, as I also do."[1] Much time had now elapsed since those two friends had been associated together in this "work of the Lord;" many new circumstances must have occurred to put the character of Timotheus to a severe trial; the confidence, however, of the Apostle had not been diminished, but rather increased. The relationship remained the same as it had been when they were formerly together at Corinth, and when the Gospel was preached among the Corinthians — to use his own words in the second Epistle — "by me and Silvanus and Timotheus."[2] And if in this anxious wish that his friend should be exposed to no *fear* there is an indication of some timidity of temperament in Timotheus, such a circumstance brings us nearer to him in sympathy, while it helps us to appreciate more fully the affection which was felt towards him by St. Paul.

We have seen that the Epistles to the Corinthians enable us to trace a considerable amount of the occupation of Timotheus on this journey, while St.

[1] 1 Cor. xvi. 10. [2] 2 Cor. i. 19.

Paul was outward bound. We can also detect his presence with the Apostle at Corinth, the farthest point of the journey; for in the Epistle to the Romans, written there, we find, "Timotheus my work-fellow saluteth you."[1] We have no means of similarly illustrating the homeward route; but at Ephesus, or in Macedonia, or at Corinth, we feel almost sure that he must have met Apollos and Titus, as well as Aquila and Priscilla;[2] and when we see the Apostle moving eastward, we find him expressly associated with a large group of companions. "There accompanied him into Asia Sopater of Berœa; and of the Thessalonians, Aristarchus and Secundus; and Gaius of Derbe, and Timotheus; and of Asia, Tychicus and Trophimus."[3] How long this large apostolic company continued to travel together we do not know. Some of them were probably trustees for the collection which St. Paul had been gathering for "the poor saints at Jerusalem."[4] Sopater of Berœa, or Aristarchus and Secundus of Thessalonica, may have returned back to Macedonia from the neighborhood of Ephesus. It is very likely that Tychicus remained there, and possible that Timotheus with Gaius went together to their native neighborhoods of Derbe and Lystra. We have no means of deciding the question. All that we know is that he is not mentioned at any subsequent part of the voyage. Nor is he specified in the account of that commotion which took

1 Rom. xvi. 21.
2 See 2 Tim. iv. 19.
3 Acts xx. 4.
4 Rom. xv. 26.

place at Jerusalem immediately after the Apostle's arrival. Trophimus, who had been one of the company at Troas, is named; he was the innocent cause of St. Paul's trouble and suffering;[1] but the name of Timotheus appears nowhere. Nor is he spoken of during the time of the imprisonment at Cæsarea. So that we are not able in any way to associate him in our thoughts with Felix or with Festus.

Again, on the voyage from Palestine to Rome, it appears almost certain that Timotheus cannot have been with St. Paul, though Aristarchus, another of the Troas party, was with him.[2] Neither on the slow progress from Cæsarea to Myra, nor in the haven on the south coast of Crete, nor on board the ship during the storm, nor in the shipwreck, nor during the three months in Malta, nor on the fine and rapid sail from Malta to the west of Italy, does St. Luke find any occasion for mentioning Timotheus. It is natural to conclude that he was not present. But we know from the Epistles that he soon rejoined his friend in Rome. In the opening of the letters to the Colossians and Philemon, the two names appear linked together,[3] just as had been the case in those earliest letters sent from Corinth to Thessalonica. Then it was "Paul and Silvanus and Timotheus." Now it is "Paul and Timotheus." Silas is not associated with St. Paul as formerly; but the close link between him

[1] Acts xxi. 29.

[2] Acts xxvii. 2. See Col. iv. 10; Philem. 24.

[3] Col. i. 1; Philem. 1.

and Timotheus subsists unbroken by lapse of years and by change of circumstances. And may we not say that the union of these names in the beginning of these letters denotes not only similarity of sentiment, but community of action, if not a certain kind of official connection? Other companions are mentioned in the letters, Demas for instance, and Luke himself; but they only send a message of Christian love near the close;[1] their signatures are not prefixed to the writing in the formal sending of "grace and peace." So preëminent is the confidence placed in Timotheus by St. Paul.

The same remark applies to the Epistle to the Philippians, which belongs to the same imprisonment. But here a passage occurs of so much importance, that it must be quoted at length. "I trust in the Lord Jesus," says the writer, "to send Timotheus shortly unto you, that I also may be of good comfort, when I know your state. For I have no man like-minded, who will naturally care for your state. For all seek their own, not the things which are Jesus Christ's. But ye know the proof of him, that as a son with the father, he hath served with me in the Gospel. Him therefore I hope to send presently, so soon as I shall see how it will go with me."[2] Very full and varied information regarding the character of Timotheus is given to us in this passage. He is contrasted with others, as being thoroughly like-minded with the Apostle, as having a true and

1 Col. iv. 14.

2 Phil. ii. 19–23.

entire sympathy with him, and as being one who could take an honest and genuine interest in the best prosperity of the Philippians. It is implied, too, that he is very different from others, who seek their own advantage, and not the honor of Christ; and it is asserted that he had always shown the utmost obedience to the Apostle in all that related to the Gospel, being to him as a son to a father: and the Philippians are directly appealed to, as *knowing*, by what they had seen themselves, that this was perfectly true.

Such is the character which we can read in the Epistles written during St. Paul's first imprisonment, and sent by Onesimus and Epaphroditus, with whom we are sure that Timotheus must have conversed often and earnestly. There remain the Epistles written to Timotheus himself in a subsequent period, of which we need not attempt to furnish the details. Whatever journeys by land or voyages by sea filled up this concluding space of the great Apostle's life; whatever privations or difficulties Timotheus himself may have then incurred,[1] one thing is very plain, that he was always at his master's service, ready to stay wherever he might be stationed, ready to go wherever he might be sent. "I besought thee to abide at Ephesus, when I went into Macedonia;" this is the language of the first Epistle. "Do thy diligence to come shortly unto me; do thy diligence to come before winter;" this is the language of the second.[2] Still it is the same relationship, of a son to a father. Still

[1] See Heb. xiii. 23.

[2] 1 Tim. i. 3; 2 Tim. iv. 9, 21.

there is the same obedience on one side, still the same confidence on the other. "My beloved son," is the phrase of one Epistle. "My own son in the faith," is the phrase of the other.[1] How great was the trust reposed in Timotheus is evident from the commissions which these letters convey. He is to repress false doctrine, to regulate public worship, to ordain faithful ministers, and, above all, to be an *example* "in word, in conversation, in charity, in spirit, in faith, in purity." [2]

And as, in all records of friendship, it is not anything connected with the discharge of public or official responsibilities which leaves the most abiding and definite impression on the mind, but usually some slight incidental circumstances that indicate the presence of a deep undercurrent of personal feeling, so, in the present instance, the mention of common details, such as might occur in the correspondence of any two friends, comes to our aid, enabling us quite easily and naturally to give the last and most characteristic touch to our picture. "The cloak that I left at Troas with Carpus, when thou comest, bring with thee, and the books, but especially the parchments." [3] Even in this there is something which seizes strongly on the imagination. We should be glad to know what those books, what those parchments were. But another passage of the same kind attracts us still

[1] 1 Tim. i. 2; 2 Tim. i. 2. [2] 1 Tim. iv. 12.
[3] 2 Tim. iv. 13.

more. In the midst of very serious injunctions, the thought of the delicate health of Timotheus and of the danger into which he might fall of neglecting one of his means of usefulness, seems to occur to the affectionate Apostle, and he says, "Drink no longer water, but use a little wine for thy stomach's sake and thine often infirmities."[1] We might with benefit use this passage as an indication of the temperance of Timotheus, and thus as an example to ourselves. Though of a delicate constitution, inherited, perhaps, from his mother, and though liable to weakness, and suffering often from fatigue, he was strictly abstemious. But here the quotation is adduced simply to illustrate the personal intimacy which subsisted to the end between the Great Apostle and the dearest of his Companions.

At the close of this survey of St. Paul's Companions, one thought remains in the mind, which is well worthy to keep its place there, as an incitement to self-examination and an exhortation to duty. Nowhere in the whole range of Biography do we find friendship and companionship employed, on so large a scale, for the highest ends, without the alloy of selfishness or ambition. Some serious questions, such as the following, are suggested regarding *our own Companions.* "Who are these Companions? How and why have they been chosen? What is the link which binds us to them? What benefits do we

[1] 1 Tim. v. 23.

gain from them, and what benefits, through them, do we confer on others? And, whatever be the links which unite us to them, is loyal allegiance to CHRIST the one commanding bond which gives strength and sacred meaning to the whole of this Companionship?"

www.ingramcontent.com/pod-product-compliance
Lightning Source LLC
LaVergne TN
LVHW020240110826
845151LV00003B/988